First Lutheran
Church Library
035920

FLC

248.8

RAI

Rainey, Dennis

Best gift you can ever give your
parents

035920

The
Best Gift
You Can Ever Give
Your Parents

DENNIS RAINEY *with* David Boehi

FAMILYLIFE™
Publishing

Little Rock, Arkansas

The Best Gift You Can Ever Give Your Parents
© 2004 by Dennis Rainey. All rights reserved.

No part of this publication may be reproduced, stored in a retrieval system, or transmitted in any form or by any means—electronic, mechanical, photocopying, recording, or otherwise—without the prior written consent of the publisher.

2004 Published by FamilyLife, a division of Campus Crusade for Christ.

ISBN: 1-57229-630-5

The present work is an abridged version of two previous works: *The Tribute* © 1994 Dennis Rainey and *The Tribute and the Promise* © 1994 Dennis Rainey.

Author: Dennis Rainey, with David Boehi
Editor: Amy L. Bradford
Editorial Assistants: Steve and Lisa Laube
Proofreaders: Fran Taylor, Anne Wooten
Cover Design and Interior Layout: Lee Smith
Photography: Dan Butkowski
Cover and Additional Photography: Licensed by Getty Images

Printed in the United States of America.

11 10 09 08 07 06 05 04   6 5 4 3 2 1

Unless otherwise noted, Scripture references are take from the New American Standard Bible®. Copyright © 1960, 1962, 1963, 1968, 1971, 1972, 1973, 1975, 1977, 1995 by The Lockman Foundation and are used by permission. www.Lockman.org

Tributes and Tribute images used by permission.

Dennis Rainey, President
5800 Ranch Dr.
Little Rock, AR 72223
1-800-FL-TODAY
www.familylife.com

A division of Campus Crusade for Christ

In honor of Ward and Dalcie Rainey,
who are the reasons for this book.

Contents

Editor's Preface

S ince its original publication as *The Tribute* in 1994, Dennis Rainey's book has prompted many readers to honor their parents. This book and its message have been featured on the "FamilyLife Today" radio program several times. With each broadcast, listeners' responses have testified to the book's impact.

Their stories come to us through hundreds of letters and copies of their Tributes to a dad or mom. We've read narratives from the adult children of Ward-and-June-Cleaver parents, ball-game-going parents, neglectful parents, absent parents, and alcoholic parents. Their words chart their paths through the Tribute-writing process—sometimes wandering through resentment or meandering through isolation. Usually, though, their trials pull out of valleys and peak in their obedience to God's fifth commandment: "Honor your father and your mother … " (Exodus 20:12).

And while many of these journeys end with reconciliation, not all do. But fortunately, many of these pilgrims sought not their parents' approval, but God's blessing. Their healing and their peace testify that God makes good on His promises.

These stories—the travelogues of God's courageous children—are what prompted FamilyLife to keep the book in print. We feel that by publishing it in a more concise form, it will appeal to even more readers and spur even more healing.

—Amy Bradford

Acknowledgments

Writing a book is like planting and maintaining an orchard. It requires the time, attention, energy, and commitment of skilled men and women who want to see an end product that yields much fruit. *The Best Gift You Can Ever Give Your Parents* is no different.

My friend and partner in ministry, Dave Boehi, deserves a medal of honor for his tireless service and painstaking care in helping shape this manuscript. Dave, once again, your critical eye has proved to be invaluable. I deeply appreciate the work that you did on this book and all that you do at FamilyLife.

This book would not be in your hands without the dedication and editing skills of Steve and Lisa Laube. Thank you for completing the daunting task of revising a book to one-quarter the original size, yet retaining the message it was intended to deliver. You are GREAT slashers! I didn't feel a thing!

I am grateful to God for the publishing team He has assembled here at FamilyLife, and especially to those who headed up this effort to get this book in the hands of the reader—Betty Rogers, Lee Smith, Dan Butkowski, John Stokes, and Ben DeBusk. Special kudos and a HEARTY word of appreciation go to Amy Bradford—thank you for coaching, encouraging, inspecting, trimming, flexing, cheering, and leading. This project would NEVER have occurred without you.

To Abe Martinez, Lisa DeBusk and Marla Rogers—thank you for the hours you spent reading this manuscript and providing valuable insights.

To the team that kept me going as we finished two books simultaneously—you all are absolutely awesome: Clark Hollingsworth, Janet Logan, Michele English, and Todd Nagel. Thank you for the way you serve our Savior and millions of families for eternity.

To my adult children—now numbering nine with spouses: Ashley, Michael, Ben, MK, Samuel, Stephanie, Rebecca, Deborah, and Laura. Thank you for appreciating your mom and me more than we deserve. Your lives are tributes to God!

Last but definitely not least, a giant thank you to Barbara, my partner, friend, and warrior in life. I want to tell you how much I appreciate you. Thanks for being a committed woman of God. And thank you for finishing that other book with me … you know what I'm talking about. You ARE the best!

Introduction

Are You Ready for an Incredible Experience?

In God's fifth commandment, "Honor your father and your mother … ," we find a unique message of hope and promise for our basic need to be in a right relationship with our parents.

However, we live in a culture where attitudes turn to blame rather than honor. Even the Christian community is slow to challenge that attitude and raise the standard to honor our parents.

Yet this command may be one of the most profound in Scripture. Indeed, I believe that there are penetrating and unforeseen benefits that are inextricably linked to one's obedience to this command:

* Could it be that the quality of life you experience today is directly tied to your obedience to this command?
* Could it be that obeying this commandment is an important test of your relationship with God?
* And on a broader scale, could it be that the very survival of our nation is tied to its sons' and daughters' honoring their parents?

Wherever you are in your relationship with your parents, whether it's great, okay, strained, or estranged, there is hope and encouragement for you in these pages.

It is found in what I call a "Tribute"—a formal document or composition that publicly proclaims your gratitude for what your parents did right, for the positive qualities and values they passed on to you.

I have gone through the process of writing Tributes for my own parents and have heard many stories over the years from others who have done the same. You will find some personal stories throughout the book that people have shared with me, and they are used with permission. If I use first names only, I have changed some details to allow people to remain anonymous.

❧

Writing a Tribute may be one of the most profound, mysterious, and incredible experiences of your entire life.

❧

I am convinced that taking an honest look at your relationship with your parents, working through any issues there, and then seeking to honor them by writing a Tribute may be one of the most profound, mysterious, and incredible experiences of your entire life.

Touching a Nerve

How sharper than a serpent's tooth it is
to have a thankless child.
—William Shakespeare

The scene is forever etched in my mind. It was August in Ozark, Missouri. I was 18 years old and about to leave home. In a few minutes I would drive off to my dorm room at Crowder Junior College in Neosho. And here in the driveway stood Dad and Mom about to face an empty nest.

For the first time in my life, I remember feeling an enormous sense of gratitude and appreciation to these two people who had given me so much of themselves and who had so fashioned my life.

As I looked them in the eyes, the emotion rose suddenly in my throat. I moved to embrace them. I swallowed hard, fought off the tears and said, with a breaking voice, "Mom, Dad, I love you."

It is tough to admit that it was the first time I remember saying those words to my dad and mom.

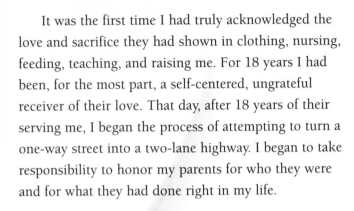

> *We have failed to train our youth in what it means to honor their parents. It is as though the fifth commandment has become the "forgotten commandment."*

It was the first time I had truly acknowledged the love and sacrifice they had shown in clothing, nursing, feeding, teaching, and raising me. For 18 years I had been, for the most part, a self-centered, ungrateful receiver of their love. That day, after 18 years of their serving me, I began the process of attempting to turn a one-way street into a two-lane highway. I began to take responsibility to honor my parents for who they were and for what they had done right in my life.

The Forgotten Commandment

My parents' humanity and their mortality became more and more real to me during college. I wrote some long letters to them expressing my praise and thanks. I also used every opportunity when I was home to look Mom and Dad in the eyes and tell them I loved them.

When I was working with teenagers, one of my favorite messages that I gave was titled "How to Raise Your Parents." Actually I camouflaged the real message behind the title, which was "Honor your father and your mother … ."

As I spoke to those teenagers I realized that I was touching a raw nerve. Some had such difficult relationships with their parents that the command to *honor* them presented a challenge of immense proportions, a major step of faith.

Since 1970, I have worked with youth and families, and I have come to this conclusion: We have failed to train our youth in what it means to honor their parents.

2   DENNIS RAINEY

It is as though the fifth commandment has become the "forgotten commandment."

A Painful Lesson

Over the next few years, when speaking to adult audiences on honoring their parents, I realized that God has something in this commandment that we are missing today. He wants to do something in our relationships with our parents that I can't even begin to understand.

One young man handed me a note that affirmed the message of honoring parents. He wrote:

> I appreciated your talk today. It brought back some memories I have about my dad that I would like to share with you. Every day that I can remember, my dad took me and hugged me and kissed me good night. Every night he verbally told me he loved me.
>
> My dad died four years ago when I was a freshman in college. I was with him the night he died. That night he hugged me and kissed me and told me he loved me, and I was too embarrassed to tell him that I loved him.
>
> He died of a heart attack two hours later after I went to bed. I remember standing over his body saying, "Dad, I love you." But it was a couple of hours too late.

As I spoke about honoring parents, I would share practical ways to demonstrate that honor. But I began to sense there had to be something more substantive than a monthly five-minute phone call—more significant than a kiss or a hug, and more effective than a Mother's Day card. Over time I began to discover—somewhat by surprise—what this "substantive honor" might look like, but I wish that I had known sooner.

A Superficial Sketch

Just a couple weeks earlier, Dad and Mom had visited us in Little Rock, Ark. After they left to go back home, I told Barbara it was one of the best times I'd ever had with Dad.

Two weeks later the phone rang. It was my brother telling me that Dad had died of a massive heart attack.

He was gone. There were no warnings, no good-byes.

In the years that followed, I reflected on my Dad's funeral. Sixty-six years of life were summed up in a 30-minute memorial. It was meaningful for our family, but it still bothered me a bit—it seemed too brief a remembrance for all he meant to us.

Dad was a great man. Impeccable character. Quiet. Hardworking. The most influential man in my life. It didn't seem right that a man's life could be summarized with such a superficial sketch.

I wondered, *Did he really know how I felt?* I had worked hard to express my love to him for several years, but words seemed so hollow. Had I really honored him as I should?

I pledged then that I would not wait until Mom died to come to grips with her impact on my life. I resolved to let her know about my feelings for her.

What I had in mind had to be personal.

So I began working on a written Tribute to my mom. I jotted down memories. Tears splattered the legal pad as I recounted lessons she had taught me and fun times we had shared. It was an emotional catharsis.

Setting Apart Words of Honor

When I finished it, I decided something was needed to set these words of honor apart from all the letters I had written in the past.

With Barbara's help, I decided to have the Tribute typeset and framed, making it into a more formal document. I took the finished product and mailed it home to Mom.

I knew she would like it, but I was unprepared for the depth of her appreciation. She hung it right above the table where she ate all her meals. There was only an old clock on another wall in that room—and that clock was no rival for my mom's Tribute.

She shared it with family, the television repairman, the plumber, and countless others who passed through her kitchen. And now I share it with you. You can read my Tribute to Mom at the end of this chapter.

My only regret in regards to Mom's Tribute is that I mailed it to her. Years later, Barbara personally read her Tribute to her parents. Seeing that emotionally poignant moment with her parents unfold at Christmas was unforgettable. I wish I had driven home to Ozark to read my Tribute to Mom—and to cry together with her.

The results of honoring my mom with a Tribute were so encouraging that I began to challenge others to write Tributes of their own. "Your parents need a tangible demonstration of your love now. Why wait until after they die to express how you feel?" I asked.

I never presented this idea as a magic potion or cure-all for healing difficult relationships. Yet, as people began implementing it, I started to see that honoring parents with a Tribute touched a deep nerve. There really was more to this command to honor parents than I realized.

I want you to welcome this process. The relationship between a parent and child is both strong and fragile. More than any other human relationship, your relationship with your parents has shaped who you are today. My guess is that, as you work through the process of writing a Tribute, you will learn as much about yourself as you do about them.

A Special Word to Children of Abusive Parents
As I continue to examine the concept of honoring parents, my experience tells me that you probably fit into one of the following categories:

Group One: Those who have good relationships with their parents
Group Two: Those who have difficult relationships with their parents
Group Three: Those who have been severely damaged by their parents

I have devoted one chapter specifically to those who have been abused. If you are someone who has been deeply wounded by severe physical, emotional, or sexual abuse by one or both of your parents, please read chapter 13 now. Then, let me gently encourage you to read through this book with an open heart and to ask God to show you how He would like you to respond. I have no desire to give you a burden that you are unable to face right now.

My Tribute to My Mom

In the winter of 1984, I wrote my Tribute to my mom. From that time forward our relationship began to change. Increasingly, I returned portions of the grace and forgiveness she had given me a thousand times as I grew up. I found myself encouraging her and lifting her spirits more than I had in the past. I related to her as a peer and started to care for her needs rather than just expect her to recognize mine.

Here is the Tribute that hung over her kitchen table for so many years (my Tribute to my dad is on page 126).

She's More Than Somebody's Mom

When she was 35, she carried him in her womb. It wasn't easy being pregnant in 1948. There were no dishwashers or disposable diapers, and there were only crude washing machines. After nine long months, he was finally born. Breech. A difficult, dangerous birth. She still says, "He came out feet first, hit the floor running, and he's been running ever since." Affectionately she calls him "The Roadrunner."

A warm kitchen was her trademark—the most secure place in the home—a shelter in the storm. Her narrow but tidy kitchen always attracted a crowd. It was the place where food and friends were made! She was a good listener. She always seemed to have the time.

Certain smells used to drift out of that kitchen—the aroma of a juicy cheeseburger drew him like a magnet.

DENNIS RAINEY

There were green beans seasoned with hickory-smoked bacon grease. Sugar cookies. Pecan pie. And the best of all, chocolate bonbons.

Oh, she wasn't perfect. Once when as a mischievous 3-year-old, he was banging pans together, she impatiently threw a pencil at him while she was on the phone. The pencil, much to her shock, narrowly missed his eye and left a sliver of lead in his cheek … it's still there. When he was 5 years old, she tied him to his bed because he tried to murder his teen-aged brother by throwing a gun at him. It narrowly missed his brother, but hit her prized antique vase instead.

She taught him forgiveness, too. When he was a teenager she forgave him when he got angry and took a swing at her (and fortunately missed). The most profound thing she modeled was a love for God and people. Compassion was always her companion. She taught him about giving to others even when she didn't feel like it.

She also taught him about accountability, truthfulness, honesty, and transparency. She modeled a tough loyalty to his dad. He always knew divorce was never an option. And she took care of her own parents when old age took its toll. She also went to church … faithfully. In fact, she led this 6-year-old boy to Jesus Christ in her Sunday evening Bible study class.

Even today, her age doesn't stop her from fishing in a cold rain, running off to get Chinese food, or wolfing down a cheeseburger and a dozen bonbons with her son.

She's truly a woman to be honored. She's more than somebody's mother … she's my mom. Mom, I love you.

~ Un Tributo a Mami ~

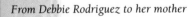

From Debbie Rodriguez to her mother

DENNIS RAINEY

CHAPTER 2

What Is Honor?

What is honored in a land will be cultivated there.
—Plato

Who receives honor in our culture today? Sports heroes receive honor. If you can dunk a basketball, knock the breath out of a running back, or throw a baseball 95 miles per hour, you can make millions of dollars in contracts and endorsements.

Entertainers receive honor. Hardly a week goes by without an award show for musicians, or television and movie performers.

Soldiers and policemen earn medals for acts of courage and heroism. Workers often are honored for top performances or for years of service to a company.

And what usually accompanies the honor? Pomp and pageantry. A pedestal. An ovation. Applause. Photographs. Handshakes. Hugs. Public recognition and words of appreciation. Tears. Prestige. Feelings of significance.

Have you ever watched someone receive an honor he was not expecting? You'll see shock, gratitude, and appreciation streak across his face.

Yet, think about who does *not* receive much honor in our culture: those in authority. We have declared open season on authority figures. Our leaders have become easy prey for sitcoms and the evening news.

In the process, we model for the succeeding generation how to dismantle and disgrace one another. We encourage the ravenous human appetite for ripping others apart. Dishonor takes us down a path that is populated with the unwelcome guests of disgrace, despair, and hopelessness.

We have become a nation of dishonor. And no nation—or person—ever moves forward in an atmosphere of dishonor.

Honor: A Weighty Matter

The verb "honor," according to *Merriam-Webster's Collegiate Dictionary,* means "to regard or treat with honor or respect."[1] However, when God commands, "Honor your father and your mother," He provides some additional meaning. In the original Hebrew language the word for "honor" meant "to make weighty."

Its literal meaning was "to lay it on them." Today, when we use this phrase—"lay it on them"—we typically mean flattery. Not so here. To honor someone meant, "I weigh you down with respect and prestige. I place upon you great worth and value." That, in fact, is what a Tribute accomplishes—"weighing down" a parent with honor, respect, and dignity.

DENNIS RAINEY

It is fascinating to observe how God used the concept of honoring parents as one of the foundational elements in forming Israel into a nation. Think of the setting: God had brought this nation of people, held captive for so long in Egypt, into the wilderness of Sinai. He had promised them the land of Israel, but up to this point He had never given them any written directions. They needed a constitution that would teach them how to relate to God and how to live with one another. They needed instructions to govern their behavior and preserve their identity as a nation.

God gave them the Ten Commandments. And to best appreciate the significance of the command to honor parents, note where it fell:

- ❋ "You shall have no other gods before Me.
- ❋ "You shall not make for yourself an idol, or any likeness of what is in heaven above or on the earth beneath … . You shall not worship them or serve them; for I, the Lord your God, am a jealous God … .
- ❋ "You shall not take the name of the Lord your God in vain … .
- ❋ "Remember the sabbath day, to keep it holy … .
- ❋ *"Honor your father and your mother, that your days may be prolonged in the land which the Lord your God gives you"* (emphasis mine).
- ❋ "You shall not murder.
- ❋ "You shall not commit adultery.

* "You shall not steal.
* "You shall not bear false witness against your neighbor.
* "You shall not covet your neighbor's house; you shall not covet your neighbor's wife or … anything that belongs to your neighbor."

—Exodus 20:3-17

God established these foundational rules for Israel— and all people—to obey. The fifth commandment may seem difficult, but soon we'll see how God helps us, so that obedience is within our reach. The key to receiving this help is our relationship with God.

Honoring parents should grow out of a strong relationship with God.

The first four commandments deal with how man relates to God. With these mandates, God establishes that He is the One who should be exalted above anyone or anything else. A nation's life—and an individual's life—is defined by its relationship with God.

Then comes the fifth commandment: Honoring parents should be a direct result of our faith in Him.

Look carefully at the commandment again. Whom did God command us to honor? Only perfect parents? Only Christian parents? Parents who are spiritually mature and insightful? Only those who never made major mistakes in rearing us?

No, God commands us to honor our parents regardless of their performance, behavior, or

DENNIS RAINEY

dysfunction. Why? Because honoring parents demands that we live by faith in God.

For some of us, honoring our parents may be a "spiritual barometer" of our relationship with God. And if we want to walk in His ways, and experience His love and power, then we need to obey His commands. In John 15:10 Jesus said, "If you keep My commandments, you will abide in My love; just as I have kept My Father's commandments, and abide in His love."

God knew we need to live by faith—to be obedient to Him without always seeing the reason or understanding the "why" for everything we do. Yes, honoring your parents may stretch your faith. You may do it only because God commanded it, not because you feel your parents deserve it. But you will grow spiritually in the process because you have exercised faith.

God ordained the "office" or position of parents so we would, in obedience, honor the office holder. The person holding the office may or may not be worthy of honor; regardless, our responsibility is to honor.

Another important truth to remember is that God did not leave us powerless to obey this commandment. Deuteronomy 30:11 states, "For this commandment which I command you today is not too difficult for you, nor is it out of reach."

No human being in history except for Christ has ever been able to obey the Ten Commandments perfectly. But God gave us the Holy Spirit, who gives us the power to obey Him. Look at Jesus' encouraging words from John 14:15-17:

"If you love Me, you will keep My commandments. And I will ask the Father, and He will give you another Helper, that He may be with you forever; that is the Spirit of truth, whom the world cannot receive, because it does not behold Him or know Him, but you know Him because He abides with you, and will be in you."

If you have received Christ as your Savior, God has given you His helper, the Holy Spirit, who can empower you to fulfill God's commandments.

Honoring parents should be a key cornerstone of a nation. By divine decree, the command to honor your parents was listed *before* the remaining directives about murder, adultery, stealing, lying, and coveting. In establishing Israel, God assigned priority status to the institution of the family and its relationships.

He makes a clear statement: Do you want your nation to live a long time? Do you want to not only survive, but to have peace in your homes and nations? Then begin by esteeming and respecting your parents.

This priority shows how it's the family—not lawmakers—that spawns and nourishes character. That's why the health and life expectancy of a nation can be measured by the way its people honor or dishonor their parents. A nation's very survival is at stake over how its children treat their parents.

Why? All of the basic components necessary for a healthy society find their origins in the family: respect

DENNIS RAINEY

and love for others, submission to authority, commitment, and character, to name a few. John MacArthur says it well:

> A person who grows up with a sense of respect for obedience to his parents will have the foundation for respecting the authority of other leaders and the rights of others in general. ... Children who respect and obey their parents will build a society that is ordered, harmonious, and productive. A generation of undisciplined, disobedient children will produce a society that is chaotic and destructive.[2]

The Warning

God thought this honor so important to the health of the nation of Israel that He commanded their leaders to put to death any child that struck or cursed his father or mother (Exodus 21:15, 17). The Lord amplified this command later in Deuteronomy 21:18-21.

The severity of a death penalty for cursing parents certainly grabs our attention. It's as if God underlined the fifth commandment and put an exclamation point at the end to say, "This is absolutely critical for your nation and its families."

In prescribing such severe consequences for sin, God was shaping Israel's conscience. He was making a statement that teaching and training children to honor their parents was a divine priority for the nation.

As I look at the priority God places on the fifth commandment and its accompanying warnings, I'm astounded that the Christian community is so silent when it comes to honoring parents. This is a command of God that He wants us to take seriously.

Honoring our parents is a command to children of all ages. There is no clause that exempts the adult child from responsibility. As we shall see, the command to honor parents is just as important for an adult child as it is for a younger child still at home.

It is an attitude accompanied by actions that say to your father or mother, "You are worthy. You have value. You are the person God sovereignly placed in my life. I choose to look at you with compassion—as a person with needs, concerns, and scars of your own."

What Honoring Is, and What It's Not

Our culture typically honors youth, wealth, beauty, and athletic ability—not parents, not the elderly, not the wise or righteous. This can distort our view of what it means to honor our parents. Let me clarify what honoring our parents is not.

Honoring is not:

* Approving of parents' wrong actions or choices
* Placing yourself back under their physical or emotional control
* Endorsing irresponsibility
* Denying what they've done wrong
* Flattering them by ignoring or denying the emotional or physical pain they may have caused you or your family members

Rest assured that honoring your parents as an adult child cannot place you back under their authority. A Tribute is not written to seek their approval, but rather to obey God.

Honoring your parents means:
- Choosing to place great value on your relationship with them
- Taking the initiative to improve the relationship
- Obeying them until you establish yourself as an adult
- Recognizing what they have done right in your life and have passed on to you as their legacy
- Seeing them through the eyes of Christ, with understanding and compassion
- Forgiving them as Christ has forgiven you

Un Tributo a Papi

¡2 sí mejor ocasión para vendirte un Tributo que en la celebración en la que honramos a los Padres! Papi, cuando pienso en ti, pienso en celebrar la vida. Pienso en tu buena disposición y tu deseo de agradar a otras personas. ¡El legado que me has dejado es muy grande y valioso! Mientras crecía, vendblecer para mí, cómo amar la vida, a no tener temor de tomar riesgo ni de tratar cosa nueva, esto cuando confiaran un cierto. Me enseñaste el arte de aprender a disfrutar, divertirme, apreciar y contar como un honor el tener la oportunidad de servir a otros.

Me sonrío al recordar las muchas veces que te observaba disfrutar la vida al máximo. En mi corazón y memoria se encuentran grabada para siempre entrega de aquellos viajes alrededor de la isla en una guagua con la gente de la iglesia. Siempre querías llevarme contigo, nunca sentí que fuera un estorbo para ti. Cómo me hacías reír cuando te disfrazabas con tu amigo Walter, y a bajaba de la guagua en las plazas de los pueblos para hacer a otras disfrutar de un momento de relajamiento, risa y alegría ...Verdaderamente, mostraras como eras hacieras reír mucho a una senrita rubia que te observaba atentamente desde la ventana de una guagua en un divertido serte disfrutar cuando estaba entre gente. ¡Cómo me enseñaste a disfrutar plenamente de la vida!

Recuerdo también cuando íbamos de vacaciones y tú siempre inventabas algunas aventuras. Ir a coger juegos a Isla Verde siempre fue una gran aventura que recuerdo con mucho cariño, y cómo teníamos el tiempo para enseñarme a cómo cogerlos y cocinarlos. Un verano, en el Hotel Barranquilas, viví contigo mi primera experiencia de tu sierra por una lema en una yagüa wíca cerca de una palma, que tú misma preparaste para que no pudiéramos usar ... y hasta se tiraron con nosotros ... ¡Cómo te complacía vernos disfrutar juntos! Me encantaba también que te tiraras en la piscina con nosotros, pues siempre tomabas tiempo para jugar en el agua y tirarnos de un lado al otro de la piscina.

Recuerdo también las veces que pasaron el día en Isla de Cabra de pasadías con la iglesia. Me encantaba verte participar en las carreras que se hacían, y siempre verte ganar. Recuerdo un día que corrías tan rápido que se dañ un calambre en la pierna y mi corazón se desplomó cuando te vi tirarte al suelo y vesolurte del dolor ... pero ahís no contrarizapan tu arruinó el resto del pasadías ... siempre has buscado algo positivo para seguir adelante. También medditaste para mí que era importante cuidar de tu cuerpo y la necesidad de hacer ejercicio concienzudamente. Lo más grande es que continúas mantilando con principio para tu hoy día.

En las Navidades, estoa disfrutaba el venirte de Santa Clara para repartir los regalos en la Nochebuena. Siempre te gustaba invitar a toda la familia y a amistades. Tú alegría y satisfacción cuando te servías disfrutar a nosotros. Y tu fabulosa el Día de Reyes, donde siempre iba con nuestra a recortar la yerba y ponerla en cajitas de zapatos para que los camellos comieran cuando los Tres Reyes vinieran a dejar tus regalitos al lado de nuestra cama. Involucrate en nuestro ser aconte de imaginación y expectativa en un mundo de fantasía que te gustaba crear a nuestro alrededor. Derrochaste que ibas, esta el alma de la fiesta, con tu música de acordeón y tu alegría exponáneas contagiaba a todas aquellos que se encontraban presente.

Lo más que recuerdo cuando crecía es que siempre tuviste tu oído presto para escucharme, especialmente nuestra antigüeda a través de mis turbulentos años de la adolescencia. Siempre tuviste tiempo para escuchar mis pensamientos y mis quejas, y una vez te saliste de carrera escuchar lo que yo tenía que decir, no importaba lo descabellado que fuera. Nunca olvidaré tu cariño hacia mí y cómo me hacías sentir que estabas de mí lado y que "esa por mí". Tu maaeva optimista y positiva he enfrentar distintas situaciones muchas veces me ha servido de aliento y de guía... y tu bumildad de conocido me ha enseñado a encontrar la gracia de Dios en la vida y a mantener viva tus citurtumbre en cada ofiicio.

Siempre te has preocupen por otros y estos sienvir a las necesidades de otras personas para suplirlas, darte a otro de tu tiempo y de tus recursos, aún en momentos donde no había mucho para dar ... tu me impresende que giné Dios ha conzfín poner tu tu mano mucho ... Nunca te vi escapenendo para ti, pero il observé otros dando a otras generosamente. Al día de hoy mis hijos sienten una gran admiración por ti, al observar tu generosidad y tu estusiasmo de vivir. Siempre vuestras un adelo de estar junto a nosotros y en la compañía de aquellos que aman. Aprecia y tengo en alta estima todo lo que has hecho y hace por nosotros, pues tu amor se hace evidente diariamente en tus acciones ... Al hacernos rosgar y formar tu propia bogar, he visto tu apoyo y cariño constantemente. En convivir de guía material y espiritual, veserviel y físico siempre has sido el primero en decir "presente". Me complaca verte en el rol de abuelo y ahora siempre tratas de acercarte a mis hijos. Yo bai ganado el amor y afecto de tus nietos quienes te ven como tú "papotar", a pesar de la distancia física que para otros servicia como un distículo.

Estoy un agradecida de Dios pues ha recibida de ti un legado de amor, me has enseñado a dar de mí misma sin medir costo en ty darde, sino que tu ejemplo he procurado que germine en mí ese deseo genuino de servir a otras, aun cuando el costo puede ser alto. Más importante aún, me has marcado a mantener un corazón sensitivo hacia la voz de Dios y a procurar ser humilde de corazón. Eres para mí un ejemplo vivo de cómo una persona que ha recibida "ningún" por su legado, ha escogido sobre la redención de Dios y ha permitido que Dios combir una certeza por belleza eterna. Tú no tuviste un modelo de lo que es ser un padre, no tuviste caminos mínimas escritas en tu vida espiritual y física... Sin embargo, has escogido combrar el curso del legado para las generaciones futuras, y con tu bace grande ante los ojos de Dios y de tu hijo que tanto te admira. Cuando consideres el legado que se fue dado a ti por tu padre biológico, "un casorito vacío", y el legado que tú me has entregado a mí y a mis hijos "una berencia rica donde el amor sacrificial por otros es evidente", no maravillte ante las huellas de los dedos de Dios en el proceso de redolcar tu vida y la evidencia tiene de la obra de arte que El ha realizado en ti; y nosotros, tus hijos y nietos, seron los beneficiarios directos de tu berencia.

Papi, sé eso mí bénav y siempre lo será. Gracia por enseñarme a reír ante la vida, por mostrarme afecto y cariño cuando creía. Gracias por tu generosidad y tu bondad. Gracias por tu negar tierno en mi vida y por enseñarme a amar a otras. Más que nada, gracias por mantenerme y ayudarme a comprender por medio de tu amor, la profundidad del amor perfecto del Padre Cleisial. ¡He devon tan orgullosa de celebrar uno el mundo como mi Papi, me siento tan orgullosa de ti y tu cariño y eres maravillosaments! Y en este Día de los Padres, 15 de junio del 2003, tiendo un Tributo de Amor a ti, ¡feliz Día de los Padres!

Tu hija que te ama,

Debbie

From Debbie Rodriguez to her father

CHAPTER 3

The Promise

*When I was a boy of 14, my father was so ignorant
I could hardly stand to have the old man around.
But when I got to be 21, I was astonished at how
much the old man had learned.*
—Mark Twain

If honoring your parents is the "forgotten commandment," then the second part of the fifth commandment must be the "forgotten blessing."

Honor your father and your mother, *that your days may be prolonged in the land which the Lord your God gives you* (Exodus 20:12, emphasis mine).

Deuteronomy 5:16 adds another phrase to the promise: "and that it may go well with you. ... "

None of the other Ten Commandments has a promise attached to it. Paul even mentions in Ephesians 6:2 that this is "the first commandment with a promise."

But what does it mean? How can your "days be prolonged" by honoring your parents? In what ways will it "go well with you"? Does God actually promise we will live longer if we obey this commandment?

Yes! You can't get around what God clearly says in this Scripture. But there is one condition: *You must be obedient to God in all areas of your life.*

Deuteronomy 30 contains some pretty specific promises, and they all boil down to this: If you obey God's commandments, He will bless you and "prosper you abundantly" (v. 9). But if you disobey God, He will withdraw those benefits:

> "See, I have set before you today life and prosperity, and death and adversity; in that I command you today to love the Lord your God, to walk in His ways and to keep His commandments and His statutes and His judgments, that you may live and multiply. ...
>
> "But if your heart turns away and you will not obey ... I declare to you today that you shall surely perish. You shall not prolong your days in the land where you are crossing the Jordan to enter and possess it."
>
> —Deuteronomy 30:15-18

Do you want to live your life with the favor of God upon you? Would you like to feel the blessing and the good hand of God upon your life? Your life can be transformed by obeying this command to honor your parents.

DENNIS RAINEY

Obviously, if we honor our parents, there are the benefits of better communication, the possibility of peace with them, and greater freedom in our relationship with them. But I believe there are some hidden benefits as well.

God Delivers on the Promise

The benefits to those who respect their parents—or fallout from the failure to honor—is evident in Scripture:

- Samson dishonored his parents by lusting after a Philistine woman and going against their counsel by marrying her. His choice was his demise: He ultimately lost favor with God, and the Philistines took over and desecrated Israel.
- Ruth honored her mother-in-law, Naomi, and God blessed her with a wealthy husband, Boaz. The long-range result, though, was that she became a part of the lineage of David and an ancestor of the Savior of the world, Jesus Christ.
- Esther, who honored her surrogate father, Mordecai, ended up becoming a queen, which resulted in the saving of the Jews.
- David honored his father, Jesse, by being faithful to shepherd his father's flock, a lowly job for a boy from a wealthy family. But David ultimately became king, and Israel grew as a nation under God's favor.

Putting Away Childishness

In 1 Corinthians 13:11, Paul writes of our need to grow

up: "When I was a child, I used to speak as a child, think as a child, reason as a child; when I became a man, I did away with childish things." Paul knew that kids will be kids—they will behave childishly. But he also implied that as we grow up, we must set aside childish behavior and become mature.

In relationships, children are by nature petty, hurtful, and fault-finding. They speak rashly, rudely, and selfishly—with little thought of how their words will affect their parents.

Children think life revolves around them. They're self-righteous. They think they are always right and others are wrong, even when the evidence has declared them guilty.

Paul's challenge is to lay aside our childishness and finish the process of becoming an adult. A part of maturing as an adult is the growing realization and conviction that you are just as responsible for the relationship as your parents are. If your parents are elderly or are in poor health, you may be even more responsible than they are for your relationship with them.

One-Way Streets

For most of your first 18 to 20 years of life, your relationship with your parents could be compared to a one-way street. The "traffic" of love generally flowed in one direction: from them to you.

And it probably remained that way through high school and college. The problem with some parent-child relationships, however, is that they continue looking like one-way streets even when the child is in his 30s and 40s.

DENNIS RAINEY

The adult child fails to assume his responsibility of making the relationship a *two*-way street. A Tribute may help you begin constructing the second lane of a two-way street back to your parents.

A Rite of Passage

"I never felt that my mother treated me like an adult."

Sound familiar? How often have you or your friends echoed these words?

This statement came from Diane, who lived in the same town as her mother. Diane said, "She still treated me and my other siblings a lot like kids. I felt a lack of respect."

To Diane's mother, there was only one way to do things—her way. So over the years, Diane began to withdraw from her.

Diane's feelings began to change, however, when she heard about the idea of writing a Tribute for her parents. As she wrote, God slowly gave her a different perspective. This helped her persevere with the Tribute when she and her mother had a big argument.

"I was very, very angry with her. It was a really big decision on my part to still do the Tribute. But with my husband's encouragement, and with God giving me the courage, I did finish it, and I gave it to Mom at Christmas."

As her mother read the Tribute, she immediately broke down in tears. "I think part of the problem was that all those years, while I was feeling she didn't respect me, she didn't feel any respect and appreciation from her kids," Diane said.

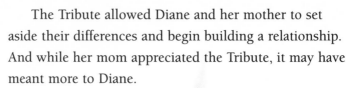

❖

*I really saw
how fruitful
obedience to
God and His
commands can
be. ... after I
did the Tribute
I felt I was
more on her
level. ... It was
a sort of a rite
of passage."
—Diane*

❖

The Tribute allowed Diane and her mother to set aside their differences and begin building a relationship. And while her mom appreciated the Tribute, it may have meant more to Diane.

"In a way, it was for me as much as for anyone else. I know it was something God wanted me to do, but I didn't know all the positive benefits that were going to come out of it. I really saw how fruitful obedience to God and His commands can be.

"It's been hard for my siblings to deal with how I handled this. They're not Christians, and they have absolutely no understanding of why I would ever look at these good things that my parents did.

"I'm not sure how to deal with that. But I do know that whereas I felt like a kid with my mom, after I did the Tribute I felt I was more on her level. I was able to relate to her more. It was a sort of a rite of passage."

Maybe you find yourself facing similar problems: you're waiting for your parents to respect you, recognize you as an adult, and let you go. But at the same time, your parents are waiting for you to honor them.

It's a standoff. Like the wife who was always waiting on her husband to act: "There's nothing I wouldn't do for him, and there's nothing he wouldn't do for me. And that's exactly what we do for each other—nothing!"

Only when we choose to take responsibility for our part of the relationship can we begin to establish ourselves as mature adults—both in our parents' eyes and our own. Let me explain.

DENNIS RAINEY

Honoring parents requires taking initiative in the relationship.
When I wrote my Tribute to Mom, something happened in me that I could not describe for years. Later, I realized the Tribute was also a formal statement that her little boy had grown up to become a man. On my own initiative I recognized her worth and value to me as her son who was now a man.

I will not suggest that the process of honoring parents with a Tribute is the total answer to a lack of self-confidence or an identity crisis in a man or a woman. Nor can I guarantee it will mark the decisive turning point in a relationship with parents.

On the other hand, I have heard and read enough stories to recognize something mysterious that happens in men and women who reach out through a Tribute and honor their parents. Perhaps it's because the act of honoring demands that we initiate and give.

As we assume our responsibility to honor our parents, we begin to change the dynamics of a relationship that may have been a one-way street. As a result, a friendship finally takes root between parent and adult child.

Honoring parents requires setting aside the "victim" mentality.
It's an old idea, but it seems to be more in vogue than ever these days: "It's not my fault!" Popular psychology de-emphasizes the concept of personal responsibility— after all, we don't want to feel guilty for the wrong choices we make, do we? Instead we are encouraged to blame others—often our parents—for our difficulties.

Let me be clear that there are many people who deserve to be called victims. I've already discussed the extraordinary impact of a parent on a child, and I certainly agree that many emotional or relational difficulties that adults face can be traced to their parents' deficiencies.

What is happening in our culture, however, is that too many people are using their victim status to avoid a prickly question: *When am I going to be responsible for my own life?*

Honoring parents helps us develop an honest and balanced view of them.
When individuals go through the process of honoring their parents, a flood of emotions surface: Gratitude. Appreciation. Joy. Love.

But other feelings well up, too: Anger. Bitterness. Disappointment over unmet expectations or broken promises. In fact, these negative emotions often hold positive memories captive.

When memories and emotions—both positive and negative—are buried, we are unable to deal with them honestly. Maturity demands that we confront our pasts. We will not experience the benefit of growing up if we deny or refuse to face the reality of having been raised by fallen human beings.

Writing a Tribute helps us face our pasts in an honest and balanced way—grieving over mistakes and pain while also acknowledging what our parents did right. For that reason, the process of writing a Tribute can bring another benefit to our lives: *healing.*

DENNIS RAINEY

CHAPTER 4

Your Lifeline to Your Legacy

What a father says to his children is not heard by the world, but it will be heard by posterity.
—Jean Paul Richter

Perhaps God wanted to establish solid links from generation to generation. Maybe that's why he calls us to honor our parents. How you relate to your parents and speak about them today can be a powerful statement of love for your children. And it allows the wisdom of one generation to pass on to another. The result is the promise of Deuteronomy 5:16: "that it may go well with you ... ."

We found that by honoring our parents, we take responsibility for the relationship—we make a two-way road out of a one-way street. And in the process we take a major step toward maturity.

I want to look at a second way it will go well with you when you honor your parents: *It allows the legacy of one generation to continue unbroken to the next.*

The Power of Legacy

By honoring your parents for their positive contributions in your life, you highlight the legacy of their lives. You bring value and dignity to human beings who may have never been successful by the world's standards. In doing so, you pass on to succeeding generations stories of lessons learned and wisdom gathered.

To explain this principle more fully, I'd like to highlight some ways honoring parents keeps a legacy alive.

Honoring parents allows learning from parents.
As I look at Scripture, it's clear to me that God's most important structure for passing along spiritual truths is the family—parents teaching their children and grandparents teaching their grandchildren, and so on. Read these words from Psalm 78:5-7:

> For He established a testimony in Jacob, and appointed a law in Israel, which He commanded our fathers, that they should teach them to their children, that the generation to come might know, even the children yet to be born, that they may arise and tell them to their children, that they should put their confidence in God, and not forget the works of God, but keep His commandments … .

DENNIS RAINEY

God calls each generation to pass spiritual truth on to the next. For the family to carry on this type of spiritual relay, they must maintain an honorable multi-generational connection.

If you read through Proverbs, you'll recognize the priority God places on the connection of children to their parents. Through this connection children learn the discipline and wisdom needed for life.

> My son, observe the commandment of your father, and do not forsake the teaching of your mother; bind them continually on your heart; tie them around your neck. When you walk about, they will guide you; when you sleep, they will watch over you; and when you awake, they will talk to you. For the commandment is a lamp, and the teaching is light; and reproofs for discipline are the way of life.
>
> —Proverbs 6:20-23

From these verses, we see that God wants parents and children to be vitally connected. He knows children are born with sinful natures, and they need to learn *wisdom, discipline,* and *obedience* from their parents.

Your parents are part of you. Their blood runs through your veins. I've counseled with enough people to realize that even when they deny it, they feel a terrible pain when they isolate themselves from their parents.

When adults do not honor their parents, they isolate themselves from two of the most important people God

I've counseled with enough people to realize that even when they deny it, they feel a terrible pain when they isolate themselves from their parents.

has placed in their lives. If you have godly parents, this is not difficult for you to understand. But if your parents are not believers, or if they have failed in their roles as parents in the past, you may have a hard time believing your parents have something to offer you.

Perhaps there isn't any spiritual legacy in your family, but is there something about God you learned from your father? Your mother? I have found even those who came from non-religious backgrounds still learned something of God's character from each of their parents.

Honoring parents allows generational connections.
Another way a legacy is poisoned through a lack of honor is when grandparents are cut off from their grandchildren.

Children should be taught to respect their elders. A part of honor is to respect their views, to try to understand them, and to refrain from challenging them in a condescending way. It could be that their ideas *are* outdated, but often their old ideas work much better than our new ones.

With this mindset, it's easy for children to pick up the attitude that old ideas are not worth considering— just because they are old. When the elderly are ignored rather than honored, when parents believe that there is nothing worthwhile their children can learn from their grandparents, then we cut ourselves off from the wisdom of the past.

Honoring your parents fosters a heritage of honor.
One of my favorite quotes to use when I'm speaking at a

DENNIS RAINEY

FamilyLife Parenting Conference concerns the downward spiral the Christian faith can take from one generation to another: "To our forefathers the Christian faith was life. To our parents it was a ritual. To us it was a necessary evil. To our children, it will be abandoned." In the same way, if you casually dishonor your parents, your children may dishonor you more aggressively.

The Legacy of Peter Loritts

Peter began his life as a slave in North Carolina. Released after President Lincoln's Emancipation Proclamation, he eventually acquired some land to farm. He never learned to read or write.

Two things were important to Peter. First, he loved the Lord. He often had his children and grandchildren read him Bible passages, which he committed to memory. And when his church needed land for a building, he donated part of his farm.

Second, he was committed to his family. He provided for them, and raised them to love the Lord. He passed on to them a heritage of honesty and integrity—and strong male leadership.

Peter's son, Crawford, was like his father in many ways. He was a man who believed in commitment and responsibility, a man who could be counted on to keep his word. If he promised something, he'd do it. He used to tell his children, "Never walk away from responsibility. You look it in its eye and you deal with it, but you don't just walk away."

Crawford grew up in the rural South in the heyday of the Ku Klux Klan. But he never allowed his children to use race as an excuse for anything. "Throughout life he would remind us to rise above that, to look beyond that," said his son, Crawford Jr. "And he would refuse to typify white people as all being the same. He had a number of white friends he worked with and shared with. And he would bring us in contact with models of people who loved us for who we were."

Crawford Jr. grew up to attend a Bible college and become a minister and radio host. Most importantly, he is a husband and also a father to four children. And he is passing on to those children the same lessons he learned from Crawford Sr., who in turn learned from Peter.

"It's funny how you catch yourself saying the same things that your dad said to you," he says. "I have two boys in sports, and I tell them, 'If you play, you stay. I don't want to hear any nonsense about you quitting because you don't like it, or because the coach yelled at you.'"

Crawford Jr. and Karen have made a special effort to pray for their children and pass on that godly heritage. They sometimes take the children up to the old homestead. "They love to sit on the porch with their grandfather and he will tell stories," Crawford says. "The sense of connectedness and destiny that gives them is absolutely incredible."

Crawford told me about how his older son, Bryan, introduced him before he spoke at a conference. "There are three men in my life who mean a lot to me," Bryan

DENNIS RAINEY

said. "The Lord Jesus, my grandfather for what he stands for, and my dad. I want to be like those three."

Peter Loritts had no grand scheme for passing on godly character from one generation to another, but that's what happened. Every person Crawford and Karen Loritts influence for Christ today is part of this godly man's legacy.

I wonder how many families have squandered a spiritual heritage by failing to honor their parents and breaking the connection from one generation to the next.

It's sobering to consider how quickly a legacy can be lost. The choice to honor is one each generation must make.

Bryan Loritts' Tribute to His Father

Like his father, Bryan has become a good friend of mine. Two years ago Crawford invited me to participate in a mentoring conference, where I had the privilege of becoming Bryan's mentor.

During the process of mentoring Bryan, it became clear that he needed to write a Tribute to his dad. I gave him my book to read, and to Bryan's credit, he went to work crafting a Tribute.

On March 26, 2004, at a black-tie event in Atlanta, a number of us surprised Crawford with a banquet honoring him for his life and ministry. At the end of the banquet, Bryan went to the podium and read Crawford his Tribute in front of 250 friends.

I wonder how many families have squandered a spiritual heritage by failing to honor their parents and breaking the connection from one generation to the next.

I recently came home from a busy weekend of ministry to discover that my younger son, Myles, had learned to walk while I was away. My heart was gripped as never before at the realization that I had missed a significant moment in his life. I had to fight back tears as I wrestled with whether or not I had failed him in some way. And so late that night, I quietly slipped out of bed and into his room, peeking down at him while he was fast asleep in his crib. As I laid my hands on him to pray, I wondered if there would be other moments, significant ones, that I would miss in his life. As never before, I felt the sometimes conflicting paths of pastoral ministry and family. While under this burden that night my thoughts were on you, Dad. Since then I've pondered one particular question: How did you bear such a burden so well?

As my mind has contemplated this question over the past months, several specific things you did have come to mind. I remember as a little boy, when Atlanta got its annual half-inch of snow, the whole city made its way to Kroger to buy milk and bread, thinking that we would all die. I was mad at you for being gone; that is, until you called. When Mom handed me the phone, you asked me what I thought you should do. I said, "Come home, Dad." You told me you were canceling your meetings to come home early ... and sure enough, you were there.

DENNIS RAINEY

I remember all those times we fished on the bank of some Georgia lake or pond. I laugh now as I think of the distinguished, world-renowned Crawford Loritts struggling to put a night crawler on a hook. But that's just it. When I was growing up, while everyone looked at you as some celebrity, I just saw you as Dad, helping me catch bream or catfish.

You taught me the importance of integrity. You would tell me over and over again that when I told someone I was going to do something to do it—after all, that's what Loritts men do. You never once made a promise to me you didn't keep. While as a child I expected to see you at my ball games (many times still in your coat and tie), as a father now I see the sacrifice you made to keep your promise and to be there. Thanks, Dad. I even remember bragging that the cashier lady at Dairy Queen gave me a dime too much in change once. You quickly turned me around, and told me to go back in and give her the dime—yet another lesson in integrity.

How you treated my mother continues to be a profound lesson in my marriage to Korie. I never once heard you raise your voice at Mom. I never saw you talk to her in a condescending way, but only in a manner that communicated the utmost respect. While divorce was the norm among my friends' parents, I never even contemplated that scenario in our home. In fact, the only time I really feared your lashing out in anger at someone was when a man in our neighborhood cursed my mother in your presence. I can still hear you say to that man, "Sir, I love Jesus; but I swear, if you come across this street, I will whup your behind."

Something tells me that, more than anything, Dad, your incredible love for Christ is what allowed you to lead your family so well. One of my earliest childhood recollections is running in on you early in the morning as you were on your knees in prayer before God. Times around the dinner table as you opened the Scriptures were where God formed in me a passion for Him and His Word. When I acknowledged this call into ministry and went off to Bible college, I can still hear your final words ringing in my ears as you prepared to leave: "Son, obey God." Dad, I'm trying.

Dad, I want to thank you for one more thing. Thank you for giving me a name that I can wear with pride. You've kept the name Loritts free from scandal, and dripping with moral purity. Wherever I am in this country, people know that name and they respect it—and it's because of your obedience to God and commitment to integrity. The late E.K. Bailey would give me a hundred dollars every time I saw him because of that name. Tony Evans and Bishop Eddie Long gave me jobs because of that name. Bishop Kenneth Ulmer has mentored and fathered me because of that name. Dennis and Barbara Rainey have profoundly influenced my wife and me because of that name. And in many regards it's that name that helps to put food on the table in my home today.

Your life has given me an incredible challenge—to live in such a way that my wife and kids can wear the name Loritts with pride as well. And by God's grace I will.

I love you,
Bryan

DENNIS RAINEY

My Soul Exhaled

Several days after the event, Bryan wrote about what he experienced to some of his friends.

I had a chance to read and present it to him Friday night, and it was probably one of the most significant things I have ever done in my life and ministry; and the most significant thing I've done by way of honoring him. He and Mom sat on stage as I read it to him, and I barely made it through due to a flood of emotions that overcame me (very unexpected). At the end he got up and we wept in each others arms.

The next day my father told me that he couldn't sleep that night and read my tribute again and cried some more. His exact words were, "You have no idea how much those words mean to me."

I feel like my soul exhaled. It's like I was carrying this burden around with me that I didn't know about as it relates to my dad, and now it's gone ... We've instantly gone to another level. We had a very good talk Saturday night, and again at lunch on Sunday. Both times I told him I loved him (now, it still doesn't feel easy or natural, but it's getting there).

Before Friday night, if my dad were to die, I would have carried a lot of guilt around for the rest of my life. Now, if he were to die tomorrow, sure, there would be grief, but there would also

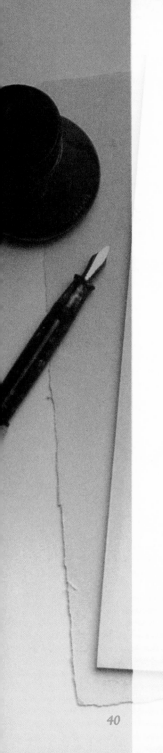

be a strong personal peace, because I took the time to honor him while he was alive.[1]

CHAPTER 5

Your Parents
Are Waiting

I was somebody once.
—Marguerite, an elderly woman in a rest home[1]

Regardless of the disposition of the child, parenting can be a drain physically, financially, mentally, and emotionally.

You can never totally repay your parents for what they gave to you. But you can try.

As with any command in Scripture, there are hidden benefits for the person who orders his life according to God's Word. The benefit here is both to us *and* to our parents.

There are two primary reasons to honor parents:

First, *the Bible declares parents are worthy of honor.* From Genesis to Revelation the Bible places a premium upon those with "gray hair." Old age was not something to be feared but a time in a person's life when they had the most wisdom to share.

> A gray head is a crown of glory; it is found in the way of righteousness.
>
> —Proverbs 16:31

> "You shall rise up before the grayheaded, and honor the aged, and you shall revere your God; I am the Lord."
>
> —Leviticus 19:32

In our youth-oriented society, the elderly are increasingly seen as a drain on our resources.

The second reason is that *honor gives parents hope and encouragement when they need it most.*

It has become very clear that parents today can suffer from an intense loneliness. Instead of reliving wonderful memories and enjoying the fruits of their child-rearing years, many parents experience an intense ache in their hearts because they no longer are vitally connected with their children.

They think back to the years when their children were young, when their children loved being with them. They wonder: Do they recognize the sacrifices we made for them?

Introspective and lonely, they wait. They may not know what they are waiting for.

So naturally, when adult children fail to recognize their parents' need for honor, it doesn't happen.

DENNIS RAINEY

That's why a lot of parents are still waiting.

If a person has to wait too long, he or can lose hope.

Honoring your parents with a Tribute can show them that some significant soil is finally being moved—soil used to construct the second lane of a two-way road back to your parents. For many, a Tribute has done just that. It has opened up the traffic to finally flow both ways. And it has been the first step toward a truly mature relationship with parents.

Parental Love

Many of us do not comprehend the remarkable power we have to bring life and happiness into our parents' lives.

The Book of Genesis tells the poignant story of what happened to Jacob when he learned that his son, Joseph, was alive. As you recall, Jacob's other sons, jealous because their father favored Joseph, sold their brother into slavery and then told Jacob he had been devoured by a wild beast. Years later they traveled to Egypt and learned that Joseph was now an important government official. Genesis 45:25-28 records:

> Then they went up from Egypt, and came to the
> land of Canaan to their father Jacob. And they
> told him, saying, "Joseph is still alive, and
> indeed he is ruler over all the land of Egypt."
> But he was stunned, for he did not believe them.
> When they told him all the words of Joseph that
> he had spoken to them, and when he saw the
> wagons that Joseph had sent to carry him, the

spirit of their father Jacob revived. Then Israel [Jacob] said, "It is enough; my son Joseph is still alive. I will go and see him before I die."

Jacob's love for his son actually restored life to his old, tired body.

Love Brings Life

I am reminded of another, more recent story I heard from a friend whose mother was dying of cancer. As my friend sat with his mother during the final hours of her life, she told him she didn't want to die until she could see her other son one last time. The problem was that this son lived 1,200 miles away.

As she uttered those words, her faraway son was in his car, pushing the speed limit to make it to his mother's side. Throughout the night, my friend stayed up with her, listening to her labored breathing. "She was breathing very shallow and very slowly. I listened all night," he recalled. "I honestly thought each breath was going to be her last."

In the morning, somehow, she was still alive. My friend heard a car screech to a stop outside the house. In rushed his brother, asking, "Is Mom still alive?"

They walked into her bedroom, and the brother leaned over his mother's face. "Mom, I'm here," he said, hugging her gently and kissing her. Weakly, she opened her eyes, smiled, and nodded. The brother turned to my friend and exclaimed, "I can't believe she's still alive!"

DENNIS RAINEY

But when they looked at her a few seconds later, she was gone. Her love helped her hold on just long enough to see her son.

The love of a child can sustain life in a parent. You have the ability to revive their lives by loving and honoring them.

The Prodigal

I think many parents can relate to the parable Christ told about the prodigal son. They know what it's like to see a child leave the home, establish independence, squander the resources given to him, and cut off communication. They feel the pain of a child who dishonors them by rejecting their values.

As I read this story in Luke 15, I'm impressed by verse 20 in which the humiliated son finally decides to return home: "But while he was still a long way off, his father saw him, and felt compassion for him, and ran and embraced him, and kissed him."

I can almost see the father looking toward the horizon several times a day, always hoping and praying his son would return. And I can feel his joy when this wayward child honors him by begging his forgiveness: "Father, I have sinned against heaven and in your sight; I am no longer worthy to be called your son" (v. 21).

Your story may read like that of the prodigal son: You actively rebelled against your parents as a teenager and never grew out of it. Perhaps you adopted a lifestyle that flagrantly communicated your rejection of their values. You've seen God change your life, but you've never asked your parents to forgive you for the way you hurt them.

It's time to start building a road back home. It's time to go home and give your parents what they need: honor … and a relationship with you. If you do, you'll benefit from it beyond measure. You have God's Word on it.

DENNIS RAINEY

Bill Barber's Tribute to His Mother

Many years ago, Bill Barber felt tension in his relationship with his mother. "We weren't getting along too well," he said. "When I was young, we were always pulling pranks on each other." As they aged, that was no longer the case.

After he read my book, he decided to honor his mother with a Tribute. He chose to keep it simple.

Apparently, the Tribute made an impression. In the years before his mother died, she lost her ability to speak—but not to point. Whenever a visitor would come to her bedside, she pointed to the Tribute that hung over her bed.

Here is what her visitors read:

Thank You to Mama

Dear Mama,

Thank you for having me. I know you weren't supposed to—medically speaking—but you did anyway. And thank you for putting up with me as a little kid. And thank you for not throwing me away 'cause I blacked your little dolls' faces. And thank for staying up all night with me when I had the measles and chills and fever, and hugging me all night. And thank you for staying with me in the Scott and White Hospital when I had my knee operation. And thank you for not killing me when you caught me pouring the medicine down the sink (when I was anemic).

And thank you for taking me on a picnic one time across the river. And thank you for taking me to the air base when you worked out there. And thank you for getting me elected as "king" of the high school. And thank you for nursing me and getting me on that bus to go play in that All-Star game. And thank you for washing my clothes, especially in college. And thank you taking me to Glosserman's and getting me a new suit to wear to the homecoming dance, and thank you for understanding about my many girlfriends.

And thank you for nursing me when I passed out in front of Joske's while you were buying Charlotte's wedding dress. And thank you for visiting me in the hospital when I had a wreck and I was so bored I flipped boogers on the ceiling.

And thank you for understanding me when I played post office [an old kissing game] and told about it. And thank you for the time you put salt in the sugar bowl on April Fool's Day. And thank you for understanding when I wouldn't wear a tie to Charlotte's wedding.

And thank you for coming to stay with us when we had Clay and Bob. And thank you for coming to stay with us when Jean had rheumatic fever and then rheumatoid arthritis, and then when Bob had his finger operated on.

And thank you for always just forgiving me and Jean and our boys for all faults and sins and overlooking things. And thank you for laughing at the world no matter what, 'cause I learned it too, and I have you to thank. Amen.

With love,
Your Son, Bill

CHAPTER 6

Making Room
for Honor

Y ou may feel the desire to honor your parents, but
you also come up with a host of justifications for
not doing it:

* "Yes, this would be good for me to do …
  sometime."
* "When my parents earn my honor, then they
  can have it."
* "I'm not good with words."
* "My parents will be critical of me."
* "We just aren't an emotional family."
* "My parents will use this to manipulate me."
* "They'll just use this to say, 'See, we were
  right—we were good parents!'"
* "They've never given me their approval—why
  should I give them mine?"

- "Honor them … after all they've done to me? You've got to be joking!"

Perhaps you need to take a close look at your heart—in the same way I did many years ago as a college student. For a number of years I had compartmentalized God in my life, allowing Him to rule only small portions of it. But after several spiritually apathetic teenage years, I finally began to grow spiritually.

Cleaning House: Inviting God Into Every Room

That year I read a booklet by Robert Boyd Munger, *My Heart—Christ's Home,* which had a profound impact on my life. It challenged me to give Jesus Christ full access and authority over every "room" in my heart—every area of my life. I recall opening some dirty rooms and dark closets that I had sealed and declared off-limits to God all my life.

This simple booklet helped me confront different areas of my life that I had hardly been willing to think about. In the same way, you may need to examine your life to determine what would prevent you from honoring your parents.

I'd like to lead you to several rooms of the heart—rooms that many people have declared off limits. Perhaps it's time to unlock those doors and allow Christ in.

The Room of Lost Convictions

We cannot deny the truth of the commandment to honor our parents. But putting it to work in our hearts is another matter.

So often we live as though God doesn't exist, or if He does, He certainly has no real claim on our lives. We have no real, practical religion of the heart. As a result we have no convictions or commitments. And without commitment, a relationship will wither and die.

The same applies for our nation and her relationship with God. As a nation we no longer believe in absolutes. We have forgotten the spiritual values that shaped our country. In fact, we have jettisoned our system of beliefs because they got in the way of having a good time.

I'm reminded of the phrase that is repeated in the Book of Judges, which described a nation that also had no absolutes: "Everyone did what was right in his own eyes" (Judges 21:25). Beliefs, or the absence of them, do shape our behavior. Convictions create a conscience, a core that repels temptation and compels us to do what is right.

If you've lost your convictions, perhaps you need to open the closet door and find the ones that matter. The Ten Commandments were given to be a tutor to remind us and convict us of what's important—that we need God—and we're not good enough to get into heaven (see Romans 3:21-30). Our first conviction should be to acknowledge our need for God and to trust the One Who can cleanse us, redeem us, and bring us back to Him—Jesus Christ.

The Room of Improper Attachment to Parents

Bill Cosby provided a glimpse into the mind of a parent when he addressed the graduating class of almost 3,000 students at the University of South Carolina. He said,

"All across this great nation, people are graduating and hearing they are 'going forth.' My concern is whether they know where 'forth' is. The road home is already paved. 'Forth' is not back home. We love you and we are proud of you, and we are not tired of you ... but we could get tired of you. 'Forth' could be next door to us, but you pay the rent."[1]

God designed the family as a place where children are nurtured and then, at the appropriate time, are released by their parents. If we as adult children are to finish the process of growing up, then we must leave (Genesis 2:24).

To continue being dependent on Mom and Dad for emotional nurturing, approval, or financial support dishonors them. And for married couples, it undermines the marriage relationship. Whether parents like it or not, they are not to have the weight of a dependent adult child in their old age—unless, of course, there are unusual circumstances, such as mental impairment or an extreme physical handicap.

For single adults, the process of leaving usually isn't as clearly defined as it is for those who marry. There is, however, a distinct point in which a single adult must assume responsibility for his own life, independent of his parents. It may occur upon graduation from high school or college, in taking a job, or at some other point; but the time comes when he or she must honor Mom and Dad by becoming independent of them.

The Room of Desire for Revenge

For some children, the only revenge available to pay their parents back for perceived or real mistakes is to withhold love and honor. Their attitude is, "I won't honor my parents until they earn it." Like a torture chamber in the basement, this room is a place of punishment, filled with bitterness.

Do you harbor any anger toward your parents? If so, what are you angry about? Their character flaws or yours? You may secretly enjoy "punishing" your parents. At some point, you will need to decide whether you will allow Christ to come into this room with His holiness, mercy, and grace. He can fill this room with release instead of revenge, love instead of bitterness.

The Room of Fear

I have seen the fear of honoring parents in the eyes of those I have counseled. It's real. It's powerful. It's controlling.

Fear is an emotional pain that can create paralysis in relationships. The door on this room is big, heavy, and foreboding. This room isn't easily opened.

Some of you may fear what honoring your parents will cost you. Honor exacts a price, perhaps in money or time, but mostly in our emotions. In abusive situations, that price may be facing a pain so deep it just doesn't seem worth it.

Barbara and I were enjoying lunch with some out-of-town friends, Charlie and Linda. The casual mood of the lunch changed abruptly when I asked Linda if she had ever written a Tribute to her parents. I will never forget

Linda's expression. She teared up. Her face flushed. She began to cry quietly, and her husband's hand gently touched hers knowingly.

I apologized immediately, but she assured me through her tears it was okay that I had asked the question. She went on, "I just can't honor them yet. The pain is just too great."

People like Linda may be afraid of a parent because of past abuse and pain that they haven't worked through. Perhaps they are afraid of their own emotions, of losing control in rage and anger. Perhaps it's the fear of having to take responsibility for their own feelings. Whatever the case, the fear is real and it is powerful.

Another common fear is that any attempts to honor parents will be dismissed or demeaned. For some, approval is so important and so infrequently given that the very thought of doing something risky feels incredibly threatening.

If this is your situation, Jesus Christ needs to be given complete access to this room to free you from all fears. In fact, we are commanded to give Him our fears, "casting all your anxiety upon Him, because He cares for you" (1 Peter 5:7). You can do this by making a list of all your fears concerning your parents and "casting" them on Christ through prayer.

The Room of Pride

This room has a small door, but a big ego lurks inside. It's the reason many people don't honor their parents: Pride. We are not willing to humble ourselves and take

DENNIS RAINEY

responsibility for how we've offended our parents in the past—through neglect, passivity, rebellion, or cruel statements. It's far easier to blame another than it is to prayerfully look inward and ask, *How have I offended my parents? How has my attitude been wrong?* I urge you not to let these unanswered and unaddressed questions keep your relationship with your parents from deepening. Genuine humility can bring healing to an estranged relationship with your parents.

Let Jesus Christ replace your ego and be Lord of this room and your life. You will find, like I did, that when Christ becomes Lord of your life, your entire heart begins to function like God created it to.

The Room of Unfair Expectations

In most hearts, there is a room filled with longings, desires, and unmet expectations. We know people aren't perfect, and nobody can be. But there's something in us that desperately wishes that our parents could have been perfect and met all of our needs.

The result is we are disappointed with our parents and don't believe we can honor them. Larry Crabb puts it well in his book *Inside Out:*

> Many of us have wonderful parents, and I do, for whom we are deeply grateful. But all of us long for what the very best parent can never provide: perfect love … No parent measures up to those standards, yet our heart will settle for nothing less. And because every child naturally

turns to this primary caregiver for what he desperately wants, every child is disappointed.[2]

Some of us need to acknowledge our unreal expectations and disappointment. We need to admit that we may be judging our parents unfairly. Most important, we need to turn to God for that perfect love that we need so much. He is the only perfect Father we'll ever have.

The Room of Selfishness

As children, we are by nature takers instead of givers. This nature continues into adulthood when we refuse to take responsibility for our relationship with our parents. We may think it just takes too much effort, but our parents need us to become givers.

Jesus' words bring focus to the issue of self-centeredness and honoring parents in Mark 7:6-13:

> "Rightly did Isaiah prophesy of you hypocrites, as it was written, 'This people honors me with their lips, but their heart is far away from Me. ... ' Neglecting the commandment of God, you hold to the tradition of men. ... You nicely set aside the commandment of God in order to keep your tradition. For Moses said, 'Honor your father and your mother'; and, 'He who speaks evil of father or mother, let him be put to death'; but you say, 'If a man says to his father or his mother, anything of mine you might have been helped by is Corban (that is to say, given to

DENNIS RAINEY

God),' you no longer permit him to do anything for his father or his mother; thus invalidating the word of God by your tradition which you have handed down. … "

In those days, some Pharisees performed a peculiar ritual before visiting their parents: They would pause between the gate and the front door and put their hands on their billfolds and declare, "Corban!" This term meant that all their money was dedicated to God and was unavailable to meet any of their parents' physical needs.

The issue, according to Jesus, was that they had nicely set aside the commandment of God in order to keep their tradition. Basically, they were selfish—they did not want to have to care for their parents. Perhaps our excuses for failing to honor our parents are not religious, but I wonder if Jesus isn't putting His finger on the core issue today—our selfishness.

No, we don't say "Corban" in our churches today, but we do have traditions that can invalidate the command of God. A nice card on Mother's Day can become a counterfeit for our failure to call Mom or go see her regularly. A costly tie for Dad may be a stingy substitute for pursuing a relationship with him. We can give our expensive, pious gifts while staking our hearts with a "No Trespassing" sign.

In our hearts, we long to have relationships with our parents like the meaningful, deep relationships we have with our closest friends. But many of us are unwilling to give our time, energy, and thoughts for the sake of our relationships. Nevertheless, this is one relationship that *will* extract a sacrifice.

DENNIS RAINEY

CHAPTER 7

The Gift of Understanding

*Christians are like schoolchildren who like to look
at the back of the book for the answers
rather than go through the process.*
—Soren Kierkegaard

Many of us call home and talk to our parents—
but how many of us really *know* the people
on the other end of the line? As self-absorbed
children, we study and analyze our parents for our own
selfish purposes. We know a lot *about* them, but we've
never sought to *understand* them.

In order to honor your parents, it's important for you
to give them three gifts: the gift of understanding, the
gift of compassion, and the gift of forgiveness. I begin
with the gift of understanding because many people have
found it to be the key to unlocking their ability to honor
their parents.

Many of us
barely know
our parents,
let alone
understand
the grief we
may have
caused them.

Proverbs 24:3-4 tells us, "By wisdom a house is built, and by understanding it is established; and by knowledge the rooms are filled with all precious and pleasant riches." If you have difficulty relating to your parents, or if your parents have hurt you in some way, you may need to step back and look at them in a fresh way—as *people*. By looking at your parents more objectively, by seeing them through the eyes of Christ, you may be able to understand more clearly why your problems with them are occurring.

At the same time, you also may gain some insight into your own shortcomings as their child—and how your failures have affected your parents. Many of us barely know our parents, let alone understand the grief we may have caused them.

As we moved through our teenage years and into adulthood, most of us began to see our parents as human beings with their own unique weaknesses and blemishes. And because of our natural bent toward the negative, it was easy to focus our 20/20 vision on the mistakes they made. At this critical crossroad many adult children make the wrong choices. Rather than seeking to understand and honor our parents, we judge and condemn them.

Understanding our parents will move us from rejecting them for their mistakes toward honoring them for what they did right. When we see them as people with needs just like ours, we are compelled as their children to reach out and give back just a portion of the love they have attempted to give us.

DENNIS RAINEY

Take a fresh look at your parents. Take a careful gaze. What do you see? Do you see people who experience worry, insecurity, fear, disappointment, and anger—just like you?

Sometimes it is easy to forget that within an elderly parent beats the heart of a small child, a teenager, a parent, and a frightened and helpless human being who desperately needs love and care.

The following poem makes a powerful statement about human needs:

Look Closer

What do you see, nurse, what do you see,
Are you thinking when you look at me—
A crabbed old woman, not very wise,
Uncertain of habit, with faraway eyes?
Who dribbles her food and takes no reply
When you say in a loud voice,
    "I do wish you'd try!"

Who seems not to notice the things that you do,
And forever is losing a stocking or shoe?
Who, resisting or not, lets you do as you will
With bathing and feeding, the long day to fill?
Is that what you're thinking,
    is that what you see?
Then open your eyes, nurse, you're not looking at me.

I'll tell you who I am as I sit here so still.
As I move at your bidding, eat at your will …
I'm a small child of ten with a father and mother,
Brothers and sisters who love one another;
A young girl of sixteen with wings on her feet,
Dreaming that soon a love she'll meet;
A bride at twenty my heart gives a leap,
Remembering the vows that I promised to keep;
At twenty-five now I have young of my own
Who need me to build a secure, happy home;
A woman of thirty, my young now grow fast,
Bound together with ties that should last;
At forty, my young sons have grown up and gone,
But my man's beside me to see I don't mourn;
At fifty, once more babies play round my knee,
Again we know children, my loved ones and me.
Dark days are upon me; my husband is dead,
I look at the future, I shudder with dread.
For my young are all rearing young
        of their own,
And I think of the years and the love
        that I've known.
I'm an old woman now and nature is cruel;
'Tis her jest to make old age look like a fool.
The body it crumbles, grace and vigor depart;
There is a stone where I once had a heart.

But inside this old carcass a
        young girl still dwells,
And now, again, my embittered heart swells,

DENNIS RAINEY

I remember the joys, I remember the pain,
And I'm loving and living life over again,
I think of the years, all too few, gone too fast,
And accept the stark fact that nothing can last.
So open your eyes, nurse, open and see
Not a crabbed old woman,
Look closer—see me!

—Phyllis McCormack[1]

Take a close, careful look at your parents. What do *you* see?

When we move toward understanding our parents, we are well on the way to honoring them. You can tell when you are beginning to understand your parents: Their behavior toward you may not change, but you will find that you don't react to them in the same ways as before. You will find it is easier to give them grace because you view them differently. You have some understanding of them and their needs.

I had to continue growing out of my childish self-centeredness and my desire for my parents to meet my needs. As I began to understand what their needs were, I was prompted to move toward them and to want to meet those needs.

For many adults, this new understanding naturally leads to the next step of honoring—the gift of compassion.

Jeff Schulte's Tribute to His Mother

Six children remember September 23, 1966, well. It was the day their mother decided they would be a family. Having returned from a meeting with her now ex-husband, who had abandoned her and her children nine months before, Marjorie determined to pull her family out of their current downward spiral. So she gathered all six children around her and announced, "With or without your dad, we will be a family."

She also made an amazing commitment: that she would provide for her family, but not at the expense of being a mother. She decided that, no matter what, she would be at home when her kids returned from school, and she would be involved in their lives.

At night, she would lie in bed and cry out to a God she hardly knew at the time, "Please help me raise these children. I can't do it on my own."

And God answered her prayers. Against great odds, her children have grown up to be solid, responsible adults today with families of their own.

On Christmas Day, 1989, each of her six children presented her with their repective parts of their Tribute to her. Following is the fifth part, from her son Jeff. Another segment, from her daughter Judy, closes chapter 8.

DENNIS RAINEY

We Will Be a Family

Part V

The Bible speaks of the importance of parents training their children to live wisely. Wisdom is defined as skill in everyday living. You have taught me how to live skillfully. I have especially noticed since I've been out on my own how so much of what I do I don't even think about. I just do it because I saw it done by you: managing money, making the most of little, taking care of my belongings, fixing things, learning by doing, working hard.

In addition to teaching me practical things, you gave me a heart. You modeled and entrusted to me a set of values that I look forward to passing on to the next generation. There is no way you could have done much for yourself all those years since most of all your energy was saved for us. I want you to know I benefited from each unselfish decision you made on my behalf. It couldn't have been easy much of the time. But you were, and still are, always there for me.

My memory takes me back to those tough, lonely years in grade school. How many nights would I come home crying? You always held me and loved me. You knew me, and I could really be honest with you about how I felt. You even stood behind me when, after two years of being teased, I broke my fist on a classmate's head.

Thanks for all the times you spanked me, made me sit in a chair, or washed my mouth out with soap. Because your

word was good, I never doubted that you were going to follow through with what you said you were going to do. As a result, I learned that there were real consequences for wrong behavior and I needed to take responsibility for my actions.

When Dad left home some 23 years ago, there were so many things you could have done. You could have turned inward—feeling sorry for yourself. You could have become angry—inevitably taking that anger out on us. You could have given up—blaming Dad for all our problems and leaving the "world" to raise us in its mold. But you didn't.

I believe God has His hand upon your life. Just look at what He has done in and through you. To God be the glory—our family is a miracle. The Lord told the apostle Paul in 2 Corinthians 12:9, "My grace is sufficient for you, for power is perfected in weakness." Paul's response was, "Most gladly, therefore, I will rather boast about my weaknesses, that the power of Christ may dwell in me." In verse 10 he continues, "When I am weak, then I am strong." Mom, because you were weak, God's grace made you strong.

The result: You are one of God's heroes. I have more respect for you than for anyone else I know. I admire you. I esteem you. I love you. And I am deeply grateful to you. I am who I am because of what God has done through you. I live every day with that thought.

I, like my five brothers and sisters, am forever indebted to you for the decision you made on September 23, 1966, to "be a family." You made us one, and by God's grace we will spend eternity as one.

DENNIS RAINEY

CHAPTER 8

The Gift of Compassion

Once an adult. Twice a child.
—a grandfather's proverb

H ere is a tremendous example of a father's compassion for his son:

No one who saw it can forget the 400-meter semifinal in the 1992 Summer Olympics. Since the previous Olympics when, plagued by a painful Achilles tendon, he pulled out a minute and a half before the race, Derek Redmond had waited for this event. In the previous two years, Derek had undergone a total of five surgeries between both Achilles tendons. He had worked hard, and his determination and intensified training were paying off. He was feeling great. He had run the first two heats in his fastest times in five years.

Halfway around the track, Derek suddenly sprawled across lane five, his right hamstring gone bad.

Redmond forced himself to his feet and began hobbling around the track. The winner of the heat had finished and headed toward the tunnel. So had the other six runners. But Derek desperately wanted to at least finish the race, so he continued to try to run.

Meanwhile, Derek's father, Jim Redmond, had made his way down the stands and onto the track. The crowd had risen to its feet, cheering the limping athlete.

At the final turn, Jim Redmond caught up to his struggling son and put his arm around him. Derek leaned on his dad's shoulder and sobbed. But they kept going. An usher attempted to intercede and escort Jim Redmond off the track, but they kept on. They crossed the finish line together, father and son.

(Adapted from Ivan Maisel's August 4, 2002, article "Derek Redmond" published in the *Dallas Morning News*.[1])

As we wonder how to give honor to our parents, we realize we will never know the internal agony *they* may have suffered in lovingly trying to help us through our rough times. I have come to see that many adults need to show the same type of compassion toward their parents that they received as children.

DENNIS RAINEY

In the same way, understanding our parents should lead us to "put on a heart of compassion" (Colossians 3:12) and then take specific steps to demonstrate that compassion to them.

Compassion is love in action. If understanding involves looking at your parents through the eyes of Christ, then compassion involves responding with the heart of Christ.

Reasons for Being Compassionate

To help us "put on a heart of compassion" toward our parents, we need to look at them from a different vantage point. As adults ourselves, we can more fully identify the struggles of parenthood.

First, parents need compassion because *raising children is an exhausting and difficult process.* Barbara and I are glad we did not have a smaller family, but our children may never know the price it cost their mother and me. In general, being a parent is demanding when it's done right. And 99 percent of the energy expended in the process will never be remembered by our children.

Second, *some children have brought great and deep pain to their parents' lives.* I have watched parents age at an accelerated rate when dealing with a rebellious child who has rejected them and their values. The rebellion can even be so subtle that it seems insignificant to outsiders, but within the family, it creates agony and deep pain.

Author and speaker Josh McDowell told of his older brother's rebellion against his parents and how it affected his mother: "Once I came home when I was a senior in high school and Mom was crying. Weeping. I asked her, 'What's wrong?' She said, `Your father and your brother have broken my heart and all I want to do is live until you graduate, then I just want to die." Two months later Josh graduated. Then his mother died two weeks later. "I blamed my brother," Josh said. "Mom died of a broken heart."[2]

The third reason parents need compassion is that, *as they grow older, they are increasingly unable to meet their own needs.* They just cannot do what they used to be able to do. And that is a significant adjustment to make. Your parents may grieve over their limitations. They may become angry over their aging. They need your compassion and your friendship to ease the pain of their physical and mental deterioration.

The final years of a parent's life constitute a terrible and wonderful irony. Your parent is an adult, full of experience and wisdom. Yet with each passing year, this adult steadily becomes more dependent on others. He feels trapped while watching his body wither. If he lives long enough, he may become totally unable to care for himself.

When the aging parent enters his final years, the adult child discovers that the roles have reversed—the parent is now totally dependent on the child. If that child lacks compassion, he will resent this new responsibility and may become bitter at being forced to rearrange his life to meet the needs of this parent.

The sacrifices that define compassion for an aging parent can frustrate and interfere with your life and family. However, these actions become a bit easier when

DENNIS RAINEY

you offer the third and final gift—forgiveness. This gift is costly, but the reward is peace—peace that can make "acting in love" fluid and sincere.

The Gift of Compassion

The gift of compassion means:

* Meeting your parents at their point of need
* Giving your parents a blessing instead of an insult
* Praying for your parents' spiritual needs and being available with an answer when the time comes

Judy Schulte's Tribute to Her Mother

Marjorie Schulte committed to fully support and fully rear her six children after her husband abandoned the family. The following Tribute, this part by her daughter Judy, testifies to her success. If you haven't done so already, you can read her story on page 64.

We Will Be a Family

Part VI

I wish at times that you could know my heart because it's difficult for me to put into words the depth of love I feel or the emotion that wells up inside me when I think of what you mean to me. I get frustrated sometimes trying to express how I feel because I'm not very good with words, and the best I can usually do is cry to get it out. But at least I'm able to get it out.

I have fond memories of, as a little girl, coming downstairs in the middle of the night when I was sick or had had a bad dream. You would pull back the covers and tell me to crawl in with you. No matter what the problem was, I usually fell fast asleep. And to this day, you have the most comfortable bed in the house.

Our love and friendship continued to blossom as you helped me make it through high school. When I didn't think I had a friend in the world, you were there to hold me or give me an encouraging word. And as the many tears fell from my

DENNIS RAINEY

face, I knew that you loved me and that I had at least one true friend. Even though I tried some things to fit in, resulting in disobedience and dishonesty on my part, I believe you knew deep down I was vulnerable and just wanted to be liked and accepted. I'm so thankful I never really became friends with those people because I might not be where I am today. Mom, thanks for being my friend anyway.

Now, I sit here as a mother myself, watching Jennifer grow up and feeling the tremendous love I have for her. Oh, what excitement I feel inside as she learns something new or just puts a smile on her pretty little face—or what pain I feel when she is hurt and cries. I feel helpless, and the only thing I can do is hold her tight in my arms just as you did with me.

I just went in to look at Jennifer tonight, and she called out my name in her sleep. I stood there realizing the love I have for her and hoping I could be the kind of mother she needs, one that will love her through thick and thin and be there for her always, as you were for me.

I would consider it a blessing to have as good a relationship with my children as I have with you. I look forward to staying up late with them talking; going to their ball games; being their biggest fan, as you were mine; and holding them close through good times and bad, letting them know I'm there for them and I love them. And I know I can do those things only because I have experienced a wonderful example of what a mother should be. I am proud and thankful that you are my mom. You've been a mother and a friend, and I love you, Mom, very much.

THE GIFT OF COMPASSION

DENNIS RAINEY

CHAPTER 9

The Gift of Forgiveness

C aptain Joseph Hazelwood loved alcohol.
Although it cost him his driver's license when he
was found guilty of driving while intoxicated, he
still retained his license to command a ship—a big ship.

On March 24, 1985, under the drunken command
of Captain Hazelwood, the Exxon oil tanker *Valdez*
impaled itself on a reef in Prince William Sound, Alaska,
ripping a hole in the ship 15 feet wide. Eleven million
gallons of Alaskan crude oil gushed out and covered
more than 2,500 square miles of the ocean.

That infamous oil spill exhausted over two billion
dollars and 10,000 men and women—many scrubbing
and swabbing rocks and birds on oil-drenched
beaches—in a massive cleanup effort. Ten years later,
the environment and wildlife in the area were still
recovering. It has been impossible to contain the impact
of that man-made disaster.

In the same way, some parents have steered the family ship into damaging reefs. Habitually intoxicated parents, for example, have abused children, spewing anger and disruption throughout their homes. The residue of mistrust now stains miles of shoreline in their children's hearts.

Cleanup campaigns in the heart are costly and can take years of effort. Even then, the impact can't be overcome fully. The damage is felt for a lifetime and for generations to come.

In reaction to this pain, some adult children become "environmental" extremists, blaming their parents for everything. They want to litigate each parental mistake and error. And in the courtroom of the mind, they replay, testify, and find fresh ways to prosecute these parental polluters.

In reality abusive parents *are* guilty; their actions and mistakes are indefensible. Parents are indeed responsible for their failures and abuses. But at some point children have to stop prosecuting and persecuting their parents for these wrongs.

In the end, one final gift of honor remains: the gift of forgiveness.

Scripture is clear: A failure to forgive and seek forgiveness results in an angry heart, resentment, and bitterness. Left to run their course unrestrained, these emotions will destroy a relationship.

It's forgiveness that makes long-term relationships possible. While it does not restore and reconcile *all* relationships, in many cases it gives us the hope that we

DENNIS RAINEY

can move beyond our hurt. And from there we can move forward to honor our parents.

Excuses

It's the nature of relationships: hurt, disappointment, and pain. We fail one another. Punish each other. Our parents damage us and we injure them.

Many of you may find that forgiving your parents is the critical step to establishing a new relationship with them. It may be the only way to be freed from the past so you can move ahead with your life.

There are many reasons children do not forgive their parents.

*Excuse: My parents **need** to be punished.*
The desire for revenge is a natural, human response. It's as if we respond to neglectful parents by saying, "When I had needs as a child, you weren't there. Now that you have needs, I'm not going to be there for you, either."

Often, the only way to take revenge on a person is in the way you treat him. "Sometimes our hate is the only ace we have left in our deck," wrote Lewis Smedes. "Our contempt is our only weapon. Our plan to get even is our only consolation. Why should we forgive?"[1]

This desire for revenge chains you to the past. It traps you in a deadly loop in which you are destined to repeat the events of the past again and again.

Excuse: My parents need to earn honor.
There are two problems with this attitude. First, the

parent who wounded you may never be able to repay you for the damage caused. Second, why should you give this person control over your emotions? Hannah More once wrote, "Forgiveness saves the expense of anger, the cost of hatred, the waste of spirits." You may suffer for years—emotionally and physically—waiting for repentance that may never transpire.

Someone once said, "The longer I carry a grudge, the heavier it gets." Many things can exhaust a person's resources over a lifetime, but none is more draining than anger. I can think of much better ways to spend my life than staying angry at my parents.

Excuse: My parents will use my forgiveness to manipulate and control me.
Fear is the motivator here. It is a big reason we don't work through issues. We feel so fragile that we cannot face the possibility of being hurt again. We fear rejection so much that we would rather live in fear's grip than confront those who have offended us.

Being controlled by fear is actually a failure to love. First John 4:18 says, "There is no fear in love; but perfect love casts out fear, because fear involves punishment, and the one who fears is not perfected in love."

Avoidance and separation from our parents is painful. So is rejection, which is a distinct possibility that comes with writing a Tribute. Neither is easy, but only honoring our parents—and risking the possibility of rejection— brings the peace and blessing that God gives when we obey Him.

DENNIS RAINEY

Forgiveness Frees

By breaking the cycle of bitterness and unresolved conflict through forgiveness, you also allow your relationships to start fresh. Writing a Tribute will demand that you take inventory of your relationship with your parents. If you harbor bitterness and anger, you will feel hindered in your attempt to honor them: Honor and love can be in shackles—imprisoned by anger, cemented by disappointment, and incarcerated by unmet expectations.

I'm convinced that one of God's reasons for the fifth commandment is to help us gain peace by resolving any anger we feel toward our parents. Bestowing true honor demands that we deal with these issues.

It is very difficult to honor people we've not forgiven. Our gestures are hypocritical and our efforts are stifled. I've observed this as people have worked on their Tributes. The good memories don't flow from their pens; those are stuffed deep inside, bolted in by anger.

That's why forgiving parents is not option in life— it's a part of fulfilling the fifth commandment.

Forgiveness Is Not ...

One of the reasons we don't seek to move through the process of forgiving our parents is that we have several misconceptions about forgiveness.

Forgiveness does not mean excusing or condoning someone's sin. By forgiving a parent for an evil action, you are *not* saying it was okay he hurt you.

Forgiveness does not mean forgetting a person's sin. It

does mean that when we remember the offense of another, we choose to give up the right to punish the other person. As we practice this discipline over a lifetime, the memories and the pain will lessen.

Forgiveness does not mean denying that we have felt pain, hurt, and anger. It is not hypocritical not to feel like forgiving another person. Forgiveness is an act of faith that begins as an act of the will. It will take time for your feelings to catch up and begin to fall in line with your decision to choose to forgive your parents.

Forgiveness does not mean stuffing grief. We need to admit the pain is there and begin to process that pain openly with another person. In severe cases it may be necessary to seek out a professional counselor to assist in this process.

Forgiveness does not mean instant, full reconciliation. Forgiveness requires work from only one party—you. But reconciliation requires cooperation from both parties. It happens over time, and it takes effort from both parties to restore trust. Furthermore, the process requires maturity and humility that may not be present in your parents (or you). Some people simply have too much baggage of their own to ever humble themselves to the degree that would allow true reconciliation.

Forgiveness Is ...

Now that I've described what forgiveness is not, it's time to look at what Scripture says it *is.* In Ephesians 4:31, the apostle Paul commands Christians to "let all bitterness and wrath and anger and clamor and slander be put away from you, along with all malice." Instead, Paul says, we are to "be kind to one another, tender-hearted, forgiving each other, just as God in Christ also has forgiven you" (v. 32).

General James Oglethorpe once stated to John Wesley, "I never forgive." Wesley replied, "Then I hope, sir, that you never sin."[2] In other words, if you can't forgive others, why should you expect God to forgive you?

Look again at Paul's instruction to forgive others "just as God in Christ also has forgiven you." This raises two interesting questions: Why do we need forgiveness? And, what did God in Christ do to forgive you?

In Luke 23 we see that after Christ was betrayed, after He was tried and convicted unfairly, after He was humiliated and scourged and jeered and spat upon, He finally suffered the cruelest indignity: the only perfect man who ever lived was hung on a cross. Nearby two criminals were also crucified. Below Him, soldiers mocked Him and stripped Him of His clothing. People sneered, "He saved others; let Him save Himself if this is the Christ of God, His Chosen One" (v. 35).

Yet Christ's response was incredible. Even at that moment, while suffering the most terrible abuse, He said, "Father, forgive them; for they do not know what they are doing" (v. 35).

Here are four powerful truths about forgiveness:

Forgiveness embraces the offenders. The first crucial lesson from this story is that Christ offered forgiveness to the very people who hurt Him the most. And that's not all—He offered it to them while they were still

God desired
your fellowship
so much He
took the
initiative in
forgiving you.

hurting Him. They did not earn His forgiveness. In the same way, your sins are a direct affront, an obscenity to a Holy God, and yet He still forgives you.

Forgiveness initiates. God desired your fellowship so much that He took the initiative in forgiving you. He did not wait for you to earn forgiveness. Romans 5:8 reads, "But God demonstrates His own love toward us, in that while we were yet sinners, Christ died for us."

Forgiveness gives up all rights to punish. God canceled your debt against Him. You deserve to die as the penalty for your sins. But God, knowing it was absolutely impossible for you to pay that debt, had Christ pay the penalty as a substitution for you. Colossians 2:13-14 says:

When you were dead in your transgressions and the uncircumcision of your flesh, He made you alive together with Him, having forgiven us all our transgressions, having canceled out the certificate of debt consisting of decrees against us, which was hostile to us; and He has taken it out of the way, having nailed it to the cross.

Forgiveness is based on reality. The final lesson of the crucifixion, though, is found later in Luke 23. One of the criminals hanging beside Christ recognized that He was the Son of God, and he called out, "Jesus, remember me when You come in Your kingdom!" (v. 42). Christ replied, "Truly I say to you, today you shall be with Me in Paradise" (v. 43).

DENNIS RAINEY

Jesus forgave this criminal of his debt to God, but there is one thing He did not do. He did not allow the man to escape the earthly penalty for his sins.

In the same way, forgiving your parents means canceling their debt against you personally—but it does not mean absolving them of other responsibilities. And it does not require that you have an ongoing relationship with them. Naturally, full reconciliation would be ideal, but your parents may need to work hard to regain your trust. In fact, you many need to confront them with their sin at some point and possibly set requirements for them to meet in order to restore a relationship with you.

Your role here is to deal with *your* response to your parents, not their responses to you. Romans 12:18 admonishes us, "If possible, so far as it depends on you, be at peace with all men." This means that you do not have the burden of responsibility for the entire relationship—only your part.

The phrase "so far as it depends on you" is not an exception clause. Rather, it shows your responsibility to seek reconciliation while acknowledging that the result of reconciliation is shared by both parties. This means that you may do everything 100 percent right and still not experience complete healing in the relationship. The command here is to initiate—to do what you can and do it with a sincere heart.

Just as understanding is seeing a person through the eyes of Christ, and just as compassion is feeling with the heart of Christ, forgiveness is releasing someone from his debt to you ... like Christ did for you.

Forgiveness—It Goes Both Ways

Oil spills. A parent's habitual caustic comments, a pattern of neglect, or a damaging choice like divorce.

Environmental impact. Hurt, confusion, mistrust, isolation, anger, and bitterness.

All caused by human error. All demand cleanup campaigns. All need forgiveness.

However, before I leave the subject of forgiveness, I need to point out another responsibility that you may need to confront. Children are just as capable as parents of polluting the home. In addition to forgiving your parents, you may need to approach them to ask forgiveness for your own failures.

DENNIS RAINEY

Robert Lewis' Tribute to His Parents

Robert Lewis is an adult child of an alcoholic. When he left home to go to college, he finally was able to escape the embarrassment of his father's drinking. But he could not escape the disappointment.

Later on, this became obvious as he was pastoring a church in Tucson, Ariz. One evening he was conducting a small group Bible study and asked, "What is something you would like to believe God for, but you think is just impossible?" Robert's own answer was, "For my dad to become a Christian. ... I'm not saying God couldn't do it, but it does feel hopeless."

I won't ruin the story for you (find it at www.familylife.com/tributelewis), but an astonishing turn of events brought his father to Christ within 24 hours of Robert's statement and set him on the path to sobriety.

Robert eventually moved his family to Little Rock, Ark., where he became my pastor. One Sunday he gave me the privilege of giving the sermon. I spoke on God's command to honor your father and mother, and challenged the congregation to consider writing a Tribute to their parents.

Robert remembered my message and, years later, took the opportunity to write his Tribute while on a retreat in Colorado. As he wrote, he recalled the anger, joy, sadness, and longing from his childhood and began to weep. "This flood of emotion showed I was getting in touch with a part of myself that I didn't even know was there. The closet door came open and all this 'stuff' flooded out. It

was powerful and potent. And bittersweet. … I felt the healing winds of freedom rushing within me."

When he finished, he had written a document he titled "Here's to My Imperfect Family." The title is startling. But Robert knew he couldn't paint a rosy picture of the past—his family was too honest for that. They all were painfully aware of the trials they had been through. Yet, at the same time, Robert wanted to remind them of the good things he had discovered in a fresh way.

These are the memories he began to see with new eyes.

Here's to My Imperfect Family

When I think of family, I think first of you, Mama, and you, Daddy. I will never understand the forces that drew or held you two together all these years. Clearly, it has not been easy. But, then again, I have now learned that few marriages are. Each carries its own crucible. Reflecting back as one of your three sons, it's not hard to say that our family was less than perfect. The "imperfect family" would be a much more descriptive term for our home. To be sure, we never had enough or did enough together. We fell short of many ideals.

Those things have little if any hold on me now. Instead, I frequently recall particular things that are now forever imbedded within me … things that need to be stated in writing, for they are the secret successes of my imperfect family.

DENNIS RAINEY

I am glad you never divorced. Today I do not think of a way out because you never got out. My children know about divorce from their friends but not from their family. They will grow up carrying permanency in marriage in their heritage; and though that in itself will not ensure success for them, it will help as it helped me.

I am more appreciative than ever for your sacrificial involvement and investments in me. I will never know them all, as my children will never know all of mine. But I do know some. Your presence at my school programs and Little League games is one. Responding to late-night fever and upset stomachs and crises like the "chicken bone affair"—a bone caught in the throat of a frightened third-grader—is another. I needed you, Mom, and you were there. I also remember the genuine compassion I received after being heartbroken because I had stood and watched rather than having starred in my first organized football game. And the hours you expended talking with me, exploring and surfacing my thoughts, feelings, and ambitions—how that helped!

I think of fishing at Kepler's Lake with Daddy. Boy, was that fun! I still enjoy it every time I relive it in my mind. And through your help for a young black man named James, I have a deeper social consciousness toward those "not like me." And thanks, Daddy, for saying "I'm sorry" when you wrongfully hit me in anger one day. You don't remember the incident, I know, but I do. It's deep inside me now—and it comes back to me every time I need to say those words to my children and my wife. Seeing that day in my mind makes the humbling process easier.

I owe both of you a thousand "thank you's"—for Florida vacations at the Driftwood Lodge … for all the oysters I could eat on my birthday … for the constant encouragement during my teenage years … for teaching me about inner toughness. I can still hear you saying, "If you can't take it, you can always quit" … for struggling in December to give Christmas its real meaning. Mom, I get the picture now … for teaching Sunday school at Trinity … for traveling to all those ball games … for standing behind me when I turned down LSU … for saying "I love you" because I needed to hear it … for the new car in college (I now know somewhat how that must have hurt financially) … for not panicking when it seemed your son had become a religious fanatic … for letting me know the financial "ride" was over after college and I was on my own … for not getting too involved in shaping my direction.

There is much more, of course. Much more. I guess if I were offered one wish, it would be for one day of childhood in time past … when I could again be your little boy. It would be a crisp, fall evening with the smell of burning leaves and a Bearcat football game in the air. I would be outside enjoying the bliss of youthful innocence. Mom, you would be frying those oysters, and Daddy, you would be calling out to our faithful dog, Toddy, "What a dog!"

So here's to my imperfect family. One that fell short in many respects, but one whose love makes the shortcomings easy to forget. Here's to the family that never had it all together, but one just perfect enough … for me!

I love you,
Robert

DENNIS RAINEY

CHAPTER 10

Seeking Your Parents' Forgiveness

*Forgiveness is the fragrance the violet sheds
on the heel that crushed it.*
—Mark Twain

If forgiveness helps free people to experience deeper relationships, then we as children we need to realize we hurt our parents just as they hurt us. And, therefore, we may need to approach them and ask for their forgiveness. This act of humility can help crack open the rusty hinge that prevents two people from opening the heavy door that separates them.

Have you ever considered that your parents may have legitimate complaints about how you've treated them? Sometimes these offenses are small, sometimes large, but chances are that they remember them.

As adult children, we can continue hurting our parents as well. By disregarding their feelings and needs, we continue to dishonor them ... and hurt them deeply.

Some parents will find it difficult to hear the words in a Tribute if you have failed to take responsibility for your own wrong actions and attitudes.

How to Seek Forgiveness From Your Parents

For the small number of you who come from very abusive, evil situations, going to your parents to seek forgiveness might be dangerous. You'll need to seek counsel about going.

For others who have not been abused, asking for forgiveness can be intimidating nonetheless. But this step is important. Some parents will find it difficult to hear the words in a Tribute if you have failed to take responsibility for your own wrong actions and attitudes. Asking for their forgiveness may be the first step toward making your relationship the "two-way street" I described earlier.

Here are some suggestions for how to do this:

Ask God for Direction

The Bible compares us to sheep. We need to be prodded occasionally to keep us going in the right direction. Some sheep want to be told, step-by-step, exactly what to do. But only the Good Shepherd knows the intimate details of your life, your parents' lives, and your family's story. He will guide you as you go through the process. Let me encourage you to go to the Lord and ask Him for guidance and wisdom.

Ask Him to search your heart and point out where you have offended your parents. The Psalmist prayed, "Search me, O God, and know my heart; try me and know my anxious thoughts; and see if there be any

DENNIS RAINEY

hurtful way in me, and lead me in the everlasting way" (Psalm 139:23-24).

If nothing comes to mind, don't feel guilty and try to manufacture some meaningless or insignificant offense.

Ask for Forgiveness

After asking God for direction, *go to your parents and ask them to forgive you.* I would not recommend going to your parents with a long grocery list of things you've done wrong, asking forgiveness for each specific item. As I've watched adult children ask parents for forgiveness, I've observed that specific confession often isn't necessary—going back in time and restating and reliving deeply damaging events can do more harm than good sometimes.

Instead, go with an attitude of humility and honor that says, "I've been wrong in my attitude toward you, I love you and want to honor you. Will you forgive me for not being the son or daughter I should've been?"

Confessing an ungrateful heart, a rebellious attitude, or selfishness are all appropriate and can bring healing.

Two other suggestions should help you prepare to ask forgiveness of your parents:

* Don't condemn them or ask them to seek *your* forgiveness for anything they've done wrong. If that's necessary, do it another time.
* If you're planning to write a Tribute for them, make sure you ask their forgiveness days or weeks beforehand. They may need time to process and internalize any forgiveness they

grant you. This will make receiving the Tribute a richer experience—instead of an overwhelming one. Your request may be something you can handle by phone or in a letter.

Leave the Results to God

There are parents who may not be healthy enough spiritually or emotionally to grant forgiveness. The currents of mistrust may run so deep that they may wait for proof that you are sincere. Keep in mind that this step is to honor your parents and obey God; your parents may not receive your gesture, but God will. Hold to this and leave the results—including your parents' responses—to Him. You are not responsible for their response or lack of one.

The possibility of rejection may be a concern for many of you, but the vast majority of parents stand ready to forgive and move on. They want to love you, not punish you. First Peter 4:8 is a passage that describes how parents have had to handle their sons' and daughters' imperfections: "Love covers a multitude of sins."

DENNIS RAINEY

Dan Jarrell's Tribute to His Mother

Dan Jarrell's father died when he was 15, leaving Dan's mother with three teenagers to raise alone. The kids did not take their dad's death well, and Dan rebelled. He reasoned that if God would take his dad, then he wanted no part of God.

By age 18, Dan was arrested for criminal activity in narcotics. For four years, he refused to change his ways. Then he prayed to receive Christ, and his critical and rebellious attitude toward his mother began to change— but, unfortunately, the relationship grew more distant. Later he began to understand part of the reason. When he had told his mother about his spiritual rebirth, she'd seen it as a rejection of all he had learned growing up in church.

The strain grew for more than a decade. Finally, Dan decided to write and present a Tribute to his mother.

"It was a watershed in our relationship," Dan told me. His Tribute was, in his words, "full of praise and respect for the hard choices she had to make to raise three teenagers. It focused on her strengths." Here is the final product.

To Mom

I respect you, Mother, for the courage it takes to get up and keep living when everything in your world falls apart. Few women left alone with three teenagers to raise could face that reality with the steadfast determination you have shown. With wisdom beyond your experience, you refused

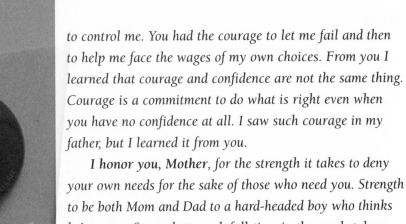

to control me. You had the courage to let me fail and then to help me face the wages of my own choices. From you I learned that courage and confidence are not the same thing. Courage is a commitment to do what is right even when you have no confidence at all. I saw such courage in my father, but I learned it from you.

I honor you, Mother, for the strength it takes to deny your own needs for the sake of those who need you. Strength to be both Mom and Dad to a hard-headed boy who thinks he's a man. Strength to work full-time in the marketplace and yet never let home be a second priority. Every morning of my life I woke up to breakfast before school. Every time I needed you, you were there. You said "no" to me, knowing I would fight you. You challenged me when I was certain to argue, and confronted me when you knew I would defend myself and accuse you of being unfair. From you I learned that strength is usually a silent virtue. Strength quietly sacrifices for the sake of higher good. It never expects honor and seldom receives it. You have shown me what it really means to be strong, and it has marked my life.

I praise you, Mother! You were faithful when many would have given up. You were flexible when many would refuse to grow and change. You were fun even in the midst of some painful times for our family. The quality of my life and the substance of my character are largely of your making. The sacrifices you made to invest in me will impact my children and my children's children. For all that you are and all you have done …

… I love you, Mom!

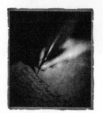

CHAPTER 11

Writing a Tribute

God gave us memory so that we might
have roses in December.[1]
—James Matthew Barrie

We live in the information age, when a flood of communication overwhelms us and trivializes many of the important things in life. In this culture, a hand-crafted, personal document can carry special power.

That's why I'm encouraging you to put together a written Tribute. It can be an island of appreciation in a sea of form letters and impersonal communications. It can allow you to express your love in a permanent, and possibly unique, way. Some of you will prefer to give a standard Tribute—one that is framed and matted. More creative types among you may opt to record your Tribute on DVD, in a song, or in some other format. Regardless, my point is that your Tribute can be recorded in any meaningful way that allows your parents to revisit it time and time again.

You will have the privilege of engraving a memory on your parents' hearts that they will never forget.

I understand that some families are hesitant to show emotion. In that case, I urge to you present your Tribute *unless* doing so would—without a doubt—actually show disrespect by forcing your will against theirs. This was the case for Todd, a single man in his 20s. His father wouldn't allow him to read the Tribute aloud. "I think it made him feel vulnerable," Todd said. "He didn't want to show any emotion."

Todd left it for his father to read and promised to mat and frame it. A year later, Todd learned how much the Tribute had meant to his father when he asked his dad what he wanted for Christmas. His dad reminded him, "Remember, you said you would put that thing you wrote in a frame?"

Your parents will probably consider it one of the greatest gifts they have ever received. You will have the privilege of engraving a memory on your parents' hearts that they will never forget.

Marble Tributes

London's Westminster Abbey is a grand structure in which thousands of people are memorialized in marble tributes and buried in the floors and walls. As I walked among those marble tributes, I couldn't help wondering why our burial stones in the United States rarely say anything about a person's life—what they lived for, their values and impact. A gravestone simply bears the name of the deceased and the date of his death. I think of what my friend Crawford Loritts says about the inscriptions on gravestones: "An entire life is summarized by a dash between two dates."

DENNIS RAINEY

Isn't a life worth more than a dash? Your Tribute may never make its way to be etched on marble or granite. But it can be etched on a heart. I encourage you to make your mark on your parents' hearts and honor them with a Tribute.

Getting Started: Set Aside Concerns of Style

At this point, you may feel a growing conviction that you need to do this. But you also may be asking yourself questions like:

* How can I write something like this when I don't know what to say?
* How can I write a Tribute if I can't remember much about my childhood?
* How can I do this if I'm not a good writer?
* My grammar and spelling are not the best.

I have found that parents don't care if you're a gifted writer, grammarian, or spelling-bee champion. They feel honored by the fact that you are speaking from your heart. So for now, set those concerns aside. To be effective, a Tribute must include emotion and a piece of your heart. You can accomplish this as you include special memories—those times of happiness, joy, celebration, and even pain and sadness that recapture how you felt as a child.

Tributes can mention specific places and events. In a way, these shared memories tell the story of your family.

Prepare Your Heart

Once you decide to write a Tribute for your parents, you should spend some time examining your heart. Take an afternoon to be alone with God. Talk with Him, read His Word and allow Him to search your heart. As Psalm 139:23-24 says, "Search me, O God, and know my heart; try me and know my anxious thoughts; and see if there be any hurtful way in me, and lead me in the everlasting way."

Take some time to meditate on the "Prepare Your Heart" section below. It includes questions that will help you discover any unresolved issues and present them to God. Journal your answers, and ask God to change your heart as He sees fit.

Prepare Your Heart

1. Are you willing to look at your parents through the eyes of Christ?
2. Are you looking to God rather than your parents for approval?
3. Are your motives pure? Are you seeking to manipulate your parents through this gesture in any way? Is giving them honor your goal? Do you expect anything in return?
4. Are you prepared to honor them regardless of their response?
5. Do you need to ask their forgiveness for anything?
6. Are you willing to forgive them for how they have hurt you?

Create a Memory List

Think back over your childhood. Can you remember a favorite vacation? A funny episode? A lesson your parents taught you? What character traits typify your dad or mom? To get started, look over the prompts in "My Memory List" below.

Some experience a very real fear they won't have anything to remember. One woman in her late 30s found her notepad nearly empty after several months of trying. Her family didn't have fun and didn't encourage family members to share openly. Two things helped her prime the pump of memories: First, her husband interviewed her by asking probing questions about her childhood. Second, she ended up taking an entire Saturday at a park to really focus. One by one the ideas came, and eventually she captured enough to write a Tribute. Presenting it was a powerful, emotional experience for her and her parents.

My Memory List
1. My favorite memory of my family is …
2. I remember that funny episode when …
3. We spent our holidays …
4. Family birthdays and anniversaries were celebrated by …
5. I treasure these character qualities in you …
6. I've adopted these hobbies, skills, and interests from you …
7. I see your personality, your habits, your sayings in me in these ways …

8. Regarding work, you've taught me to …
9. Regarding life, I grateful that you taught me …
10. Because of you, I now value …
11. I remember and treasure this bit of advice you gave me …
12. The greatest lesson you ever taught me was …
13. When it comes to parenting, I've learned these things from you …
14. You've taught me many things. Some of them that I'll pass on to my children or others include …

Write the Tribute

Now it's time to write. Don't worry about being fancy here—just tell the story as if you are talking to a friend. If you plan to honor both parents, you will need to decide whether you want to write two individual Tributes or one Tribute to both. There's no right or wrong here—it all depends on the occasion and what you feel comfortable with.

You might want to start off with a statement telling why you have written this Tribute. Then look over your memory list. This will help you capture your thoughts and statements of gratitude.

After you have written this first draft, read through it another time, looking for ways to improve it. Does everything make sense? Is the writing clear enough that another reader can understand what you are describing?

It also helps to have another person—a friend or spouse—read your Tribute. He may spot some

DENNIS RAINEY

problems you haven't thought of or catch a phrase that, while clear to you, is unclear to an outsider. If your grammar and spelling are a concern for you, ask him to suggest corrections.

At this point, you'll want to determine your format (frame and mat size, etc.). The appendix includes suggested word counts for different sizes. Account for any photos or mementos that will be included. You may need to edit your Tribute to fit within the spaced allotted.

Frame the Tribute

Now that you have finished writing your Tribute, it's time to design the gift for your parents. First, you will need to *create a clean version of the document, suitable for framing.* Here are a few suggestions:

* If you have access to a computer with word processing or desktop publishing software, set your document in the style and size you desire. Then print it using a high-quality printer.
* Have your document typeset by a local graphic designer or at a Kwik Kopy store or print shop.
* Hire a calligrapher to write your Tribute on parchment. Use a large piece of paper, and specify that the lettering be large and clear. Calligraphy can be difficult to read otherwise, especially with longer documents.
* To help preserve the document, use acid-free paper. This can be found in craft stores or wherever scrapbook supplies are sold. A solid

white or cream paper, as compared to patterned or bright papers, will match the widest selection of mat colors.

* If you choose, add photos, artwork, or other mementos. Barbara threaded ribbon and lace through the mat for her parents' Tribute. I have seen some creative Tributes that included line drawings that corresponded to the theme of the document. One Tribute began with a drawing of a twig on a tree. Next to it the first sentence read, "AS THE TWIG IS BENT and as a young child is led, so determines the direction of that life …"

* UV filtering glass will help prevent fading of the Tribute, mat, or any photos you include. A store-bought frame generally does not include this type of glass, but it can be replaced by a frame shop for a reasonable cost.

Present the Tribute to Your Parents

Here are a few ideas that will bring additional honor to your parents:

Do it publicly: This is perhaps the most effective way to make the Tribute memorable. You can present it at a special occasion such as a family reunion, birthday party, anniversary party, or when the family gathers together for Thanksgiving, Christmas, Mother's Day, or Father's Day. Since this could be an emotional time, choose a location where the honoree will not be too uncomfortable should he or she cry. A public restaurant may not be the best place for this.

DENNIS RAINEY

Or do it privately: Perhaps you will want to steal away with your mom or dad for a private reading of your Tribute. Possibly a trip home for no other reason would etch the message on their hearts permanently. You may have to pull them aside at a family gathering, like Christmas, and read it to them.

Do it with your children listening: What better picture can we give the next generation of the profound power of obeying God and His commandments?

Barbara Rainey's Tribute to Her Parents

As Barbara read her Tribute to her parents on Christmas Day in 1987, she says she found the time to be an emotional one for all three of them. They really liked the Tribute and immediately hung it up in the kitchen, where it still hangs today.

Over the years, since that presentation, Barbara has found the Tribute helped to dismantle some miscommunication that had occurred in the past. It also opened up opportunities for Barbara and her parents to enjoy their relationship even more and to see a solid friendship grow between her them.

A Christmas Tribute

One of my most vivid and pleasant memories is of us kids watching you both work and working with you. As I look back, much of the work I remember was seasonal. With Mom I remember weeding, working, and planting flower beds in the spring. Dad supervised us when he took down storm windows, and we kids got the screens and lined them up against tree trunks to be washed, rinsed, and hung in anticipation of the warm summer days to come. In the summer, there was flower-bed maintenance and lawn work to do. I remember my job was to trim the edges of the driveway and sidewalks with the hand clippers. When fall arrived there were leaves to be raked and storm windows to be returned to their protective duty. And then, as the snows

DENNIS RAINEY

came, our shovels kept the sidewalks and driveway clean.

There were inside duties as well—like cleaning sinks and learning to wash dishes the right way. Mom taught me to sew, iron, embroider, and to finish what I started. I remember being told more than once, "Anything worth doing is worth doing well." Thank you for the gift of a strong work ethic from both experience and your example.

The gifts of character and common sense are now mine because of your model. I learned to value honesty, respect for my elders, and good manners. You taught me to be conservative and not wasteful, and to value quality because it would endure.

I'm thankful to you both for the gift of self-confidence. Though my self-esteem faltered during my teen years, you demonstrated that you trusted me, and I always knew you believed in me. I remember your allowing me to do a lot with Jimmy when he was a baby and toddler. I felt at times like he was mine as I fed him, rocked him, talked and played with him, and took him to a carnival with my date when he was 3.

You also expressed trust by allowing me to express my creativity—at your expense! You let me decorate the house at Christmas, arrange flowers in the summer, and fix my room up the way I wanted. But the one that takes the cake is when you let me paint the bathroom fire-engine red with white and black trim—a thing I don't think I'd let my kids do. But I'm very grateful for that expression of trust, because it gave me a greater sense of self-confidence.

Another priceless gift was the gift of a good spiritual foundation. We faithfully attended church and Sunday

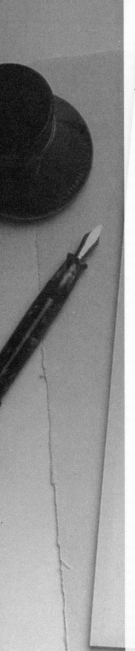

school as a family, and I was encouraged to attend Vacation Bible School in the summers and youth group in the teen years. I learned the central importance of God in my life. Because we were always there, I memorized many of the great Christian hymns that I love to this day.

Because you loved me you corrected my grammar, picked up my Kleenex, and you let me go: to France, to college, and to Dennis. Though many of the details are long since forgotten, I'll always remember how proud I felt as I walked down the aisle with Dad, and you both gave me away in marriage.

The last gift I mention is in no way the least. In fact, it is probably the greatest because it is foundational to all the others. It is the example of your marriage. I cannot recall a single argument or disagreement between you. It was apparent that you loved each other, cared for each other, and liked each other. I never felt insecure or fearful that you would leave one another or get a divorce. I treasure that gift of your good, solid, happy marriage. I attribute a great deal of the success of my marriage to the example I saw in yours.

And so, in this season of giving, some 38 years after you gave me the gift of life, I give you this Tribute. With a heart of gratitude, I give you my appreciation, my admiration, and my love.

Your daughter, Barbara
Christmas 1987

DENNIS RAINEY

CHAPTER 12

No Regrets

Even now, 21 years after my father died, not a week goes by that I don't find myself thinking I should call him.
—Herb Gardner

When I first began to speak on honoring parents, I received a letter from one of my students that put the issue in perspective:

Dear Dennis:

Your lecture today brought to mind the importance of phone calls to parents. My mother died about one year prior to my enlistment in the Air Force. As I departed New York City bound for San Antonio, my father took a day off work to see me off on my new adventure. To my knowledge, it was the only day he ever took off work, other than at my mother's funeral, and [it was] the only time I saw him cry.

I left with a promise that I would call him every Sunday at 2 p.m. and was faithful to that promise. One Sunday the phone rang for a long time and when Dad finally answered, I was truly concerned that something had gone wrong. Dad assured me all was well.

He seemed to have a lot to talk about that day. He expressed his sorrow at not having been able to spend more time with me as I grew up. I assured him that I understood and all the times we did have together were memorable and meaningful. His closing words were, "I love you and I miss you."

Those were the last words he spoke to me. Two days later I received a phone call and the voice on the other end said, "Pops is dead." It was later determined that Dad suffered two heart attacks, one conceivably on the day that I had called.

I pray that you will continue to stress contact with parents. However that contact is made, it could be the last opportunity to share your heart with someone who loved you and for you to express that the love was mutual.

(signed) A student thankful for being reminded of a two-way blessing

I like that phrase: "a two-way blessing." That's what honoring your parents is—a blessing to the parent in finally receiving thanks for what he did right and a blessing to the child who can grow old knowing no words were left unsaid.

DENNIS RAINEY

If a Parent Has Already Died

This chapter will unearth some difficult emotions for those of you who are feeling the regret of not honoring a parent before he died. As I know myself, you may never be able to erase those feelings, but I can offer two suggestions:

First, *allow yourself to grieve over the loss of your parent* and *over your failure to honor.* I can still remember sitting at my dad's funeral with deep grief, but also with immense pride in a man who was the bedrock of my early years.

It wasn't until after my dad was gone that I began to measure the man. Thirty years later I continue to take measurements, and the magnitude of what he left me looms larger in my mind.

Next, *make a special effort to honor the living parent—as a way of honoring the one who is deceased.*

By praising the man my mother chose to spend her life with, I was telling her, "Not only was your husband worthy of honor, but you are worthy as well because you made such a wise choice."

Finally, *look for ways to honor your deceased parent.* Consider that your children will benefit from knowing the legacy their grandfather or grandmother left them. A Tribute can be a permanent milestone for these young ones as they begin their pilgrimages through life.

"A two-way blessing." That's what honoring your parents is— a blessing to the parent in finally receiving thanks for what he did right and a blessing to the child who can grow old knowing no words were left unsaid.

The Coehlo siblings designed a full book of Tributes to their parents.

CHAPTER 13

When the Damage Goes Deep: Abusive Situations

My father was frightened of his father, I was frightened of my father, and I am damned well going to see to it that my children are frightened of me.
—King George V

If you have suffered from abusive parents, nothing I could say would adequately capture what you have felt. The idea of honoring your abusive parent and making the relationship a two-way street seems nearly impossible. Maybe your heartache is so intense that you feel I've been insensitive to your situation.

I realize not everyone came from a warm, loving home. Some parents are evil. Wickedness personified.

I realize not every person reading these pages is ready to face his abuser, let alone entertain thoughts of somehow honoring him as a parent.

I realize some parents will mock any effort to honor them. I cannot promise you a happy ending.

This is not a book about an instant, superficial cure for a deep wound caused by the abusive parent. Writing a Tribute will not magically solve your problems with your parents. Yet for the adult child who was abused by his parents, the process of honoring parents—even in small ways—may be a critical step toward healing.

I encourage you to pursue healing through the honest admission of abuse, thoughtful forgiveness, and honor of your parent. It is not important that you have arrived, but that you are on the road to healing. Oliver Wendell Holmes said: "I find the great thing in this world is not where we stand, but in what direction we are moving." The fact that you're reading this book indicates some movement and some desire—however faint or clouded by anger—to pursue the healing that God can bring you. Congratulations for having stepped on this road. I urge you to keep moving in this positive direction.

Moving Toward Honor

Why is moving to honor parents an important process for an abuse victim? I can think of several reasons.

God calls his children to obedience.

Humanly speaking, it doesn't seem fair to command those who have been victimized emotionally, physically,

DENNIS RAINEY

or sexually by their parents to honor them. But because the Bible is God's truth, and because it shows us how to live, we must obey Him and His commands.

Many abuse victims are led to believe—often by the very people who harm them—that they deserve the abuse and are somehow at fault. Nothing could be further from the truth. But the victim is responsible for something else: how he lives the rest of his life. Bitterness and rage is certainly understandable in an abuse victim, but ultimately that victim must make a decision whether to allow God to comfort and heal.

Fortunately, the God of truth is also the God of grace (John 1:14,16-17). He is the giver of mercy and grace and is patient with us as we go through life's processes.

God knows and understands your situation, and He knows that honoring those who harm you is both a choice and a process. However, you can take heart knowing that His grace is sufficient to help you do what you feel is impossible.

In the same way, God can use your limitations and your circumstances in an evil world. God would never want anyone to be abused by evil. He doesn't cause evil, but He does allow it. And somehow He mysteriously weaves His purposes into our lives through people—like us—who are fallen, depraved creatures.

The process may bring healing.
The process of honoring your parents can help move you from rage and anger, denial and ambivalence, to an honest assessment of what your parent's fault is and

I have seen
that God has
put it in the
heart of a
child to never
want to give
up on having
a relationship
with his
parents.

what your responsibility is. It ultimately moves you to a trust in a sovereign God.

As you are faithful to deal honestly and honorably with the parent who has abused you, God will reward you "that it may be well with you" (Ephesians 6:3a). The command of God to honor parents may be what it takes to help you realize the extent of your pain, move from denial, press on toward forgiveness, and to pursue parents who have damaged your life. If you masquerade behind a cloak of Christian slogans and catch-phrases, you can "spiritualize" the problem away and deny its very existence.

A friend of mine who has counseled numerous abuse victims says, "I have seen that God has put it in the heart of a child to never want to give up on having a relationship with his parents. He has an innate desire that never goes away to love his parents and have a healthy relationship with them."

The process may help reconcile a parent to God.
For some of you, the idea of honoring parents is almost laughable. You may have a parent who seems to have no redeeming value. Or you may face a situation where, in order to have a relationship in the future, you need to confront a parent about past abuse.

Many books by counselors today go through the steps that an abuse victim should take in order to confront the abuser. But few, even in the evangelical culture, seem to acknowledge the responsibility to honor even these parents.

DENNIS RAINEY

I want to make it clear that I have no problem with the concept of confronting parents when that confrontation is necessary. But it should be done with the right attitude. I believe honoring parents demands that, as you confront them, you do it with the desire to help that parent know Christ as his Savior. As Dan Allender writes in his book, *The Wounded Heart,* "The objective [of the confrontation] must be to bless the other person rather than to make sure we are not abused again."[1] I am not suggesting that you put yourself in harm's way (that is, if continuing abuse seems possible), but rather that you go to the abuser to show him his wrong (per Matthew 18:15)—*so he may repent and be reconciled to God,* not so you can seek revenge.

In the same book, Allender tells the story of a young man who confronted his father about past sexual abuse. The father denied it, and eventually the son chose to break off the relationship. You might think this is the opposite of honoring, but it isn't. You see, the son also made it clear that he was willing to begin again if the father would repent.

This is what Allender calls "bold love": making the effort to restore a person to full life. "He honored his father," Allender writes, "by giving him the opportunity to repent and taste the restoration of relationship with the righteous Father. The door to relationship was closed, but not locked."[2]

Working Through the Pain of Abuse
Here are some suggestions to consider as you begin to

work through the process. I also encourage you to talk to your pastor or a mature Christian counselor as you take these steps.

First, *acknowledge any emotional shock, fear, and anger you may have at the thought of having to honor your parents.*

Real meaning in life is found in real relationships with the one and only real God and with real people. It does not mean going with a layer of insulation around your heart to protect you from further abuse. True relationships demand risk and authenticity. I am *not* speaking of going back and placing your life under your parents' control. What I am promoting is developing an attitude where you can approach with an open heart, receptive to receive love and pain.

Next, *take an honest inventory of the extent of your abuse.* It's interesting how often we want to avoid reality. Some abuse victims pretend their families are perfect, and they are unwilling to admit or confront past abuse. Others focus solely on the negative and refuse to acknowledge that their parents may have done some things well.

Then, *as an act of your will, choose to forgive your parents for all the damage they've done to you.*

Finally, *when you are ready, go to your parents to honor them.* This for some will be the ultimate test. To be honest, I still wonder how the command to honor parents gets worked out in these different, dark situations. When I hear some people talk about what they experienced, I wonder if I would be able to forgive "seventy times seven," as Jesus commanded in Matthew 18:21-22.

DENNIS RAINEY

If you do attempt to honor your parents with a written document like a Tribute, keep your expectations in check. Go with an obedient heart, and beware of looking for a positive response. If they respond positively to your Tribute, then your relationship can begin to heal. But if they don't, ask God to enable you to fulfill the command of Romans 12:18: "If possible, so far as it depends on you, be at peace with all men."

If after an honest self-evaluation, you find that you have done all that you can, then continue your life in peace. Keep on laying aside the desire to be the avenger of your wounds. Let God handle it. In the same chapter of Romans, Paul warns and promises, "Never take your own revenge, beloved, but leave room for the wrath of God, for it is written, 'Vengeance is Mine, I will repay,' says the Lord" (v. 19).

God is bigger than your parents. You may never see how He handles it, but He will settle all accounts. He promised.

An Optional Step

Some just can't bring themselves to write a Tribute and give it to their parents. At this point I'd like to recommend an option that abuse victims may find achievable.

Try writing a Tribute that only you will read. Use the process of writing the Tribute as a way of expressing your faith to God. You may even want to write a Tribute *to* God, your heavenly Father. Perhaps the expressions of forgiveness, love, and honor that come through this private Tribute will bring healing to your soul.

A Few Cautions

Those who have been abused won't find this process easy. It will involve prayer, Scripture, counsel, and a sacrificial obedience—all of which may occur over several years. Here are a few suggestions to consider as you walk this journey.

Do not make writing a Tribute the ultimate test for your relationship with your parents. Be careful about expecting it to be a "make or break" venture. When you are ready, let it be what it is—simply one step toward honoring your parents and restoring your relationship.

Most important is what happens in your heart. Some who are in a state of denial will write tributes to their parents and never work through the feelings they have. It would be better that you prayerfully take your time than rush ahead, only to be disappointed by your parents' response or lack of it.

Be patient as you work to reclaim positive memories. It may mean you learn that your parents planted some roses, but you just can't find them—*yet.* Maybe the roses are surrounded by a thicket of thorn bushes. Those briars may have to be uprooted to reveal the roses.

Some parents will refuse to be reconnected. There are some parents who may not want to take responsibility for failures. Or maybe at this point in their lives they aren't able to assume that responsibility. Perhaps they are just mean, evil people who remain hardened—resisting your love. Undoubtedly, this conclusion will be disappointing, even heartbreaking. Give yourself time to grieve and seek comfort in Christ.

DENNIS RAINEY

Realize that God commands you to honor your parents, not their abuses. Honor the people who have been given the positions, not their evil, degrading acts. Not their wrong choices. Not their damaging, wounding acts against you.

Avoid comparison to others. For some people, taking one baby step can demand as much faith and courage as walking a mile would for someone else. A phone call to your parents may represent a huge, risky venture. The Tribute may be out of the question right now. Be obedient to take the steps God has set before you.

Use extreme caution as you seek to build a relationship with abusive parents. In some severe cases, such as habitual sexual abuse or extreme emotional trauma, you may be wise to avoid personal contact. You may also need to protect your children. And in cases like these, it's important to seek counsel.

DENNIS RAINEY

CHAPTER 14

Are You Worthy of Honor?

A good character is the best tombstone. Those who
loved you and were helped by you will remember you.
So carve your name on hearts and not on marble.
—C. H. Spurgeon

Throughout this book, I have exhorted you as a child to honor your parents. Now, I'd like to challenge you with a question that Henry Brandt posed to a group of parents. Even though it was more than two decades ago, I have never been able to escape the weight and significance of his question:

"Are *you* worthy of honor?"

What Is Worthwhile?

The content in so many Tributes seems to emphasize that grown children consider three things important:

121

I have never been able to escape the weight and significance of his question: "Are you worthy of honor?"

their parents' involvement, their parents' emotional support, and their parents' character.

Let's consider how we can become parents worthy of honor by building these qualities into our lives.

Your children will remember your involvement.
More than anything, your children want you to be involved in their lives. They need more than your time; they need your attention. They flourish when you focus on them.

It's more than just showing up at soccer games with a cell phone in your pocket. They need your heart in tune with theirs as they make their choices and hammer out their characters. They need you to know what's going on in their lives. They need you to help them think about the clothing they wear, the types of people they date, and the peer pressure they face.

In order to be a parent worthy of honor, you can't just "be there" as much as possible; you have to be *all* there.

Being involved with your children means more than just doing things with them, however. Involvement means we know what is going on in the *souls* of our children.

A Special Challenge to Dads

Many adults grew up with fathers who were good providers materially but were uninvolved in their kids' lives. Over the last few decades, too many fathers have pulled back from leadership in their families. To a large degree, we who call ourselves

DENNIS RAINEY

dads are responsible for this paralysis of character in our homes.

Too many of us are not leading our families into the battle against evil. Instead we're too passively disengaged—consumed with our careers, preoccupied with our toys and hobbies—to get involved with our kids' lives. Real men with real character act; they take responsibility head-on. They may not do it perfectly, but they tackle issues and battlefronts courageously. They are men worthy of honor.

Men, we need to hear and heed Paul's words to the church at Corinth:

> Be on the alert, stand firm in the faith, act like men, be strong. Let all that you do be done in love.
>
> —1 Corinthians 16:13-14

We've got to encourage one another to be involved and not to abandon our kids to the culture. We've got to do it because God is going to hold us responsible for how we protect our families.

Men, your hearts need to be connected to the hearts of your children. You may need to cry out in prayer. The last verse of the Old Testament, Malachi 4:6, gives us His promise: "And He will restore the hearts of the fathers to their children, and the hearts of the children to their fathers, lest I come and smite the land with a curse."

If you don't know what's going on in your kids' souls (and besides God, who can read minds?), I urge you to ask God to show you opportunities to engage with them. Ask Him to reconnect your heart to your children. He will help you to be worthy of honor and to be involved in your child's life.

Your children will remember your emotional support.
How often do you tell your children that you love them or that you've forgiven them? One woman wrote to tell me, "I told my parents many times how much I love them, and have only heard my parents tell me those words probably twice—the first at 40 years old ... [and they've] never [said] the words, 'I forgive.'" Your kids should hear these words so often that they have no idea how many times you've said them.

Another way to give your children emotional support is by using the power of the printed word. Letters and notes are tangible reminders to your children that you love and care for them. Young children especially will treasure your handwritten notes of affection.

Emotional support is also felt when we physically touch our children. Hugs, tight embraces, and kisses are all the steady practice of a parent who wishes to be worthy of honor.

Your children will remember your character.
The late Neil Postman has said, "Our children are messengers we send to a time we shall not see."[1] As a parent, what kind of message are you sending to the

next generation? Are your message and your life worthy of being emulated and being honored? What character qualities do you want to pass on to your children? What do you believe in? What are your core values?

The Roman philosopher Seneca said, "You must know for which harbor you are headed if you are to catch the right wind to take you there."[2] If you've determined what your core values are, then you can find creative ways to teach and model them to your children.

As a parent, you have the incredible responsibility of shaping the moral conscience of the next generation. Even though your children will grow up to make their own choices, the character qualities you model and teach will help mold them and give them direction. In fact, I've noticed that many children, after passing through years of rebellion against their parents, settle into adulthood by adopting many of the same character qualities they saw in their parents.

Experiencing God's Blessing

There is much about the command and promise of Exodus 20:12 that I still have yet to apply and understand. It would be my prayer that you would step into the process of fulfilling your responsibility to your parents and experience the privileges of obedience.

My prayer is that you will do what's right. That you will seek to be obedient to God by honoring your parents. And that you'll experience God's blessing as a result.

As a parent, you have the incredible responsibility of shaping the moral conscience of the next generation.

My Tribute to My Dad

I wrote a Tribute to my father nearly 10 years after he died, which I feel not only honored him, but also brought closure to me. I have no idea whether those in heaven are able to see what happens here on earth, but I do know he would have been pleased. And I am certain of this: God sees and He is pleased with the Tribute I wrote because it honors my dad.

The only thing better would have been to have read it to him in person.

A Tribute to "Hook" Rainey

"Dad's home!" I used to yell as the back door slammed shut.

Our small, two-story frame house would shudder when the back door slammed shut. The sound of the slamming door was especially loud when one man came through its threshold—my dad. I can recall, as a little boy, playing in my room and hearing that door send a series of quakes that rippled through the walls and rattled the windows. It was my dad's signature and signal that a day of work was completed and a man was now home.

I would yell, "Dad's home!" and then dash through the hall and kitchen to greet him and give him a well-deserved hug. I would then follow him like a little puppy to the washroom where he washed his calloused, grimy hands like a "real man." Everything about him signaled he was a "real

DENNIS RAINEY

man"—from the gritty Lava soap to the Vitalis hair tonic and Old Spice aftershave.

My dad was a unique blend of no-nonsense and discipline with a subtle sense of humor. He was a quiet and private man. He was a man of few words, who didn't seem to need many words to get the job done. His countenance commanded respect. In fact, there were several boys who had personality and discipline transformations when they graduated from the third-grade Sunday school class to my dad's fourth-grade class. Miraculously, discipline problems dried up along with dozens of paper spit wads. In the 12 months that followed, paper airplanes were grounded, and eight boys sat up straight in their chairs dutifully listening to the lesson.

"Hook" Rainey, they used to call him. The tall lefty got his nickname from his curve ball—a pitch so crooked it mystified batters. I got the feeling he was on his way to becoming a legend in his day—he even pitched a game against Dizzy Dean. Funny thing, but he never could remember the score of that memorable game! (I used to accuse him of convenient amnesia!)

I recall the easy chair that used to carry the shape of his exhausted form. I usually planned my assault on him as he was reading the evening paper. I'm certain I nearly pestered him to death on more than one occasion while asking my weary dad to play catch. And play catch he did. Night after night, "Hook" taught me how to throw a curve, slider, and knuckle ball. He used to claim you could count the stitches on his knuckle ball—and when he threw that patented knuckler, the entire front yard was filled with

laughter—his and mine. I always loved to hear him laugh. Somehow it told me everything was secure.

When I was 3 or so, he went hunting in Colorado and "bagged" a fierce teddy bear. He staged the "action" on film and brought the beast back to me. My kids now play with that worn-out, 35-year-old, black-and-white bear.

I watched him look after the needs of his mother—he used to visit his mom three or four times a week. He modeled what it meant to honor one's parents.

From him I learned about integrity, trust, and how to be a man of my word. His example taught me the importance of perseverance, for he stuck with his job for nearly 45 years. He leaves me an indelible imprint of sinking roots down deep—and living with the same people with whom he did business.

When I was in high school, I won the magazine sales contest because I introduced myself as Hook Rainey's son. That was a good enough reason for an instant sale for nearly 100 percent of my customers. My dad had helped so many people that being his son gave me immeasurable credibility. (For a while I actually thought I was a great salesman!)

His reputation was untarnished in the community. His funeral was attended by nearly a third of the small, southwest Missouri community. He lived and worked all within five miles of where he was born. One man was even able to say about my father, "In all my years, I never heard a negative word about Hook Rainey."

He gave me imperishable memories instead of just things: memories of Little League baseball (he was coach); fishing trips where he netted my fish, so small they went through the holes in the net; and a "clipped" collection of all the baseball and basketball scores from my games, of which he never missed one. There are memories of watching him through the frosted window of our old pickup truck delivering hams at Christmas. Memories of the feel of his whiskers when he wrestled with me on the floor of the living room, and memories of him whispering to me—an extroverted, impetuous boy—not to bother people while they work. And finally, memories of snuggling close to him as we watched the game of the week with Dizzy Dean as the announcer.

As an impressionable young boy, my radar caught more of his life than he ever knew. He was the model and hero I needed during some perilous teenage years—and you know what? He still is. He taught me the importance of hard work and completing a task. I learned about lasting commitment from him—I never feared my parents would divorce. My dad was absolutely committed to my mom. I felt secure and protected.

But most importantly, he taught me about character. He did what was right, even when no one was looking. I never heard him talk about cheating on taxes—he paid them and didn't grumble. His integrity was impeccable. I never heard him lie, and his eyes always demanded the same truth in return. The mental snapshot of his character still fuels and energizes my life today.

"Dad's home!" I can still hear the door slam and the house quake.

This morning as I write this, Dad truly is "home"—in heaven. I look forward to seeing him again someday and saying thanks for the legacy he gave me. And mostly for being "my dad."

But right now, you'll have to pardon me. I miss him.

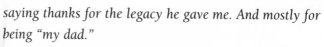

My Tribute to Dad

DENNIS RAINEY

Afterword

I want to thank you for caring enough about your relationship with your parents to read this book. Undoubtedly you have already thought of multiple ways you can honor them. God promises He will bless us if we honor our parents. I do hope at some point you'll be able to give them your Tribute. It really is worth it!

We are launching a new web page for Tributes on our website, familylife.com. Since the first edition of this book was published in 1994, hundreds of people have sent us Tributes they've written for their parents, and I invite you to do the same. For a limited time, we plan to post selections from these Tributes on a regular basis.

If you'd like to send us a copy of your Tribute, look for instructions at www.familylife.com/tribute.

Please include three elements when you send your Tribute:

* First, share some of the history of your relationship with your parents—not a lot, just enough to clarify your situation (three or four paragraphs).
* Second, describe how you gave the Tribute to your parents.
* Finally, tell about any changes that may have occurred in your relationship with your parents after you presented the Tribute.

May God bless you mightily for honoring your parents.

Appendix

Suggested Formats for Framed Tributes

Frame Size	Font Size	Word Limit
8 1/2 X 11	14 pt.	350-500
	11 pt.	500-700
8 1/2 X 14	14 pt.	500-600
	11 pt.	600-750
11 X 17	14 pt.	900-1100
	11 pt.	1350-1500
18 X 24	18 pt.	850-975
	14 pt.	900-1200

Notes

Chapter 2

1. *Merriam-Webster's Collegiate Dictionary*, 10th ed., s.v. "honor."

2. John MacArthur, *Ephesians* (Chicago: Moody Press, 1986), 312-315.

Chapter 4

1. Bryan Loritts. "Tribute." (30 March 2004). Used by permission.

Chapter 5

1. Michael S. Horton, *The Law of Perfect Freedom* (Chicago: Moody Press), page unknown.

Chapter 6

1. "Bill Cosby Has Message for Grads," *The Los Angeles Times,* 18 May 1986, 2A.

2. Larry Crabb, *Inside Out* (Colorado Springs: NavPress, 1988), 77.

Chapter 7

1. Phyllis McCormack. "Look Closer." *LenClark.com.* http://www.lenclark.com/Look%20Closer.htm (24 March 2004). Reprinted with permission by Michael E. McCormack.

Chapter 8

1. Ivan Maisel, "Derek Redmond." *Dallas Morning News,* 4 August 1992, 17B.

2. Josh McDowell, "Honoring Dad," interview by Bob Lepine, "FamilyLife Today," program #392, 10 May 1994.

Chapter 9

1. Lewis B. Smedes, "Forgiveness: The Power to Change the Past," *Christianity Today*, 7 January 1983, 22.

2. "Are You Good at Forgiving?" *Our Daily Bread*. April 2, 2001. 27 March 2004). http://www.gospelcom.net/rbc/odb/odb-04-02-01.shtml.

Chapter 11

1. The Phrase Finder. "Roses in December." http://phrases.shu.ac.uk/bulletin_board/8/messages/918.html (13 April 2004).

Chapter 13

1. Dan Allender, *The Wounded Heart* (Colorado Springs: NavPress, 1990), 179.

2. Allender, 238.

Chapter 14

1. Gwen Gross. "Unexpected Poignancy in the Sept. 11 Aftermath." *The School Administrator Web Edition*. February 2002. http://www.aasa.org/publications/sa/2002_02/Colvin_Gross.htm (27 March 2004).

2. Carol. "Quotes." *The Merry Traveler.* http://www.merrytraveler.com/quotes.htm (27 March 2004).